WOK
COOKING

This edition published in 1993 by
Tiger Books International PLC, London.
By arrangement with CLB Publishing,
Godalming, Surrey, England.
© Gräfe und Unzer GmbH, München.
Printed and bound in Italy.
ISBN 1-85501-356-8

Translated from the German edition
"Köstliches aus dem Wok"
by Andrew Wilson, in association with
First Edition Translations Ltd,
Cambridge, England.

WOK
COOKING

Angelika Ilies

TIGER BOOKS INTERNATIONAL
LONDON

Foreword

Is there anything more enjoyable than cooking for friends or family and then sitting down at table together, with all the time in the world, to eat the delicious results, listening to the exclamations of appreciation and taking the credit for a successful meal? It is particularly pleasurable on such occasions to try out new dishes, and cooking with a wok is becoming a very popular way of doing just that. This large, semi-circular pan is used to cook choice ingredients, finely chopped, in just seconds, so that everything retains its aroma and texture. Preparation is extremely simple, and nothing can go wrong, not even the first time, which of course is particularly important if you are cooking for guests. You can cook in a wok just as you would normally do in your kitchen. Don't serve the cooked food in a separate dish – surprise your guests by taking it straight to the table in the wok. However, the wok can also be used in another way for entertaining guests. You can cook a complete meal in it at the table, before their very eyes, or each person can create his or her own speciality from a variety of ready-prepared ingredients laid out in advance. To do this, however, you need a good strong spirit burner, otherwise there will not be enough heat to cook the food properly.

You can cook virtually anything in a wok. You can use it for stir-frying, deep-frying, steaming and braising. The only limits are set by your own imagination. This book contains recipes for Asian and Western dishes, most of them the sort of exotic fare typically prepared in a wok. There are also ideas for more familiar dishes: everything you are used to cooking in a frying pan or saucepan can be cooked in a wok. In order to help you buy the unfamiliar ingredients, they are described and pictured on pages 18–25. You can always omit individual ingredients if you cannot obtain them or do not like them. It is less important to have every single ingredient than it is to ensure that the ones you do use are of the best quality and carefully prepared. So enjoy reading this book, and have fun cooking in your wok for yourself and your guests.

Contents

Just as there is no such thing as European cooking, so there is no single "Asian" cuisine. Each country has its own specialities and preferences. In none of them, however, are dishes served in any particular order. There are always several dishes on the table at the same time, including delicacies with vegetables, rice or noodles, and meat, poultry or fish.

Rice is the basic food of Asia. Here, women are working in the flooded paddy fields.

China

This vast country is characterized by extreme geographical and climatic differences, so it is hardly surprising that each region favours different specialities. Peking cooking has great refinement, and is particularly varied and elegant. Flour-based products such as spring rolls and noodles are preferred to rice, which does not grow in the region. Shanghai cooking uses rice and noodles in equal proportions; fish dishes are a characteristic feature, as are soy sauce and sweet and sour dishes. Hot, spicy food is popular in Szechwan, as is anything with a powerful flavour. Rice grows in abundance here and is frequently served at table; duck and pork are more commonly eaten than fish. Cantonese cooking is influenced by the fertility of the region: tropical fruits, vegetables, meat, poultry and fish are all used in a wide variety of dishes. And it was here that stir-frying in a wok originated. In all regions, the harmoniousness and elegant shape of the ingredients used are just as important as the contrast of colours, tastes and textures. Sweet is often combined with sour, soft with crunchy, bland with spicy. Food is not too highly spiced, so that the aromas of the various ingredients are preserved. Ginger and garlic are used in virtually all dishes. Other popular ingredients include soya products such as tofu, bamboo shoots, dried mushrooms, spring onions, Chinese cabbage, various kinds of leaf vegetable, rice wine, soy sauce, oyster sauce, hoisin sauce, sesame oil, Chinese plum sauce, vinegar, dried shrimps and shrimp paste, various types of noodles, rice, coriander, turmeric, star anise, five-spice powder and Szechwan pepper.

Thailand

The majority of Thais are Buddhists and therefore have no dietary restrictions imposed by their religion. Meat is eaten, as are fish, vegetables and fruit. Hot, spicy yet light dishes are particularly popular, and rather milder dishes are served with highly seasoned sauces and dips. Limes, coconut milk and unsalted rice help to alleviate the heat of the food. Commonly used seasonings include sour ones such as lemon grass, kaffir lime leaves and tamarind, as well as garlic, shallots, coriander, galingale, ginger, basil, chilli, shrimp paste, fish, oyster and plum sauce and, less commonly, soy sauce. Pungent curry pastes prepared from a wide assortment of fresh ingredients, peanuts, various leaf vegetables, green beans, fresh fruit and fish dishes are also popular. Food may be baked in charcoal ovens, deep-fried or stir-fried in woks or gently steamed.

India

Many Indians eat no meat or fish for religious reasons and there is an abundance of vegetarian dishes in Indian cooking. In southern India in particular meat is seldom eaten. Highly spiced dishes are popular there, served with a lot of rice, vegetables and various pulses (dal). In northern India, meat and fish dishes are also cooked. Fresh spices (chilli, garlic, coriander, cumin, ginger, turmeric, cardamom, cinnamon) are used in abundance everywhere. A little water is usually added to them to make a thick, highly aromatic curry paste; this is particularly fiery in the Madras region, in the hot south of the country. Rice, coconuts and sour milk products such as yoghurt play an important role. Ghee, or clarified butter, is often used for frying. In northern India, the tandoor, a conical clay oven, has for centuries been used to cook food, often threaded on skewers and quickly baked in the oven. Throughout India, food is stir-fried in large, heavy pans.

A Chinese street dealer selling the traditional beaten metal woks and accessories.

On the floating markets in Thailand you will find everything the country has to offer.

Indonesia

Indonesia is made up of many islands, including Java and Bali, and each one has its own cuisine. There are influences from Indian and Chinese cooking, as well as from Holland and England. Knives and forks are in common use, and chopsticks are used only for stirring food. Food is cooked in woks, steamers and casseroles, with the ingredients being finely chopped beforehand. The Javanese dish nasi goreng and the sumptuous Indonesian rijsttafel are typical, well-known specialities. Fish abounds in the seas around Indonesia and is an extremely popular food. Moreover, virtually all the spices in the world flourish on the islands of Indonesia, and cooks like to make lavish use of them. The aromas of their dishes are correspondingly varied. Sambals, more or less pungent spice pastes based on peppers or chillies, are particularly popular. Palm sugar, coconut milk and sour flavourings such as tamarind paste and lemon grass serve to reduce the heat. Subtle aromas are provided by ingredients such as galingale, ginger, cloves, cinnamon, turmeric, garlic, cumin, coriander and various types of soy sauce as well as peanut and shrimp paste. Spices are often ground to a thick paste with a pestle and mortar.

Malaysia

Malaysian cooking is very similar to that of Indonesia. There are also many foreign influences here, including strong Thai ones in the north of the country. As in Indonesia and Thailand, food is cooked in a wok as well as in steamers and casseroles. The abundant use of spices means the food is very varied, with fresh fruit being used as well as all kinds of vegetables, meat, poultry, fish and rice. As in Thailand and Indonesia, spicy dishes with coconut milk are popular, as are satay, small chunks of meat cooked on skewers and served with a spicy peanut sauce.

Fresh vegetables are an important element in wok cookery.

Japan

In virtually no other country is such great importance attached to the absolute freshness of ingredients as in Japan. Only freshly caught fish can be used to make sushi (small cakes of rice topped with raw fish). Fish is generally much more popular than meat in Japan; it is eaten raw, fried or boiled. Tofu is also frequently served. Everything is combined with rice (which used to be eaten three times a day) or noodles, a lot of fresh vegetables and various aromatic mushrooms. Commonly used flavourings include green horseradish (wasabi), soy sauce, rice wine (sake) and rice vinegar, seaweed, ginger and sesame. As well as raw delicacies like sushi, the most frequently served dishes are fried or braised for the shortest possible time: in that way, the aroma and goodness of the ingredients are preserved as far as possible.

Korea

Koreans eat a hot meal three times a day, and each one is accompanied by rice, barley or millet. All the dishes are placed on the table at the same time. As in China, many of the ingredients are carefully chopped into small pieces and cooked quickly in a wok. Korean pickled vegetables are one speciality that should not be missed. Rice or one of the other cereals are combined with red beans, leeks and other vegetables, as well as meat and fish. Popular seasonings include dried mushrooms, sesame seeds, chillies, ginger, garlic and an aromatic chilli paste. Sweet foods are more popular in Korea than in most other Asian countries, and they are not only served as desserts. Fruit is often combined with spicy food, but is also served before or after a meal.

Spice markets are the places to buy the ingredients that make Asian dishes so distinctive.

Even at Asian food stalls, woks are used a great deal for stir-frying and deep-frying.

"Wok" is a Cantonese word and simply means "cooking pot". This cross between a saucepan and a frying pan was developed several thousand years ago in the Canton region of China, where fuel was scarce. There was usually only one fireplace, on which the whole meal had to be prepared. In order to make the best possible use of scarce fuel, the wok was hung directly over the fire. Its shape and the material of which it was fashioned made it a good conductor of the heat given off by the flames that flickered beneath it. All the ingredients were finely chopped before cooking, thus reducing cooking time to a minimum and economizing on the use of expensive wood. In the course of the centuries, the wok came to be used all over the Far East. Asian people everywhere have a high regard for nature, and thus for all food. They make every effort in their cooking to preserve as far as possible the aroma, colour and texture of the fresh ingredients – which is very easy to do with a wok. The wok has now begun a triumphal march around the world, and this practical cooking pot can now be bought in various forms in virtually all kitchen utensil shops.

The traditional wok

This looks rather like a hollowed-out hemisphere with a long wooden handle. It has a rounded base and sloping sides and is fashioned from beaten iron or steel. These materials conduct heat rapidly, but also cool down quickly as soon as the wok is removed from the heat. This means that food cannot overcook. It is preferable for the metal to remain slightly uneven after being beaten, since the food then clings to the edge of the wok while the liquid runs downwards. This makes it easy to bind sauces in the bottom of the wok. These classic woks can be obtained in Chinese shops and they are supplied with a metal ring that ensures stability on a gas stove. They are not suitable for electric cookers.

On the other hand, they can be used on gas stoves or good spirit burners. Every time an iron wok is cleaned, the inside must be coated with a little oil to prevent rusting.

• Woks made of cast iron are stable and robust. However, they retain heat for a long time. For this reason, food should be transferred to a serving dish immediately it is cooked. One disadvantage is that these woks are heavy. They also have to be coated with a little oil after use.

• Stainless steel woks: lighter models most closely resemble the traditional wok, while heavier ones are more similar in use to cast-iron woks. They require little care, but are extremely expensive.

• Woks designed for use on a spirit burner can be used to cook at the table. However, only large spirit burners, or multi-burner stoves, generate sufficient heat for a wok.

• Electric woks: these can also be used to cook at the table. They get hot enough for all methods of cooking. However, they are very expensive.

Preparing your wok for use

Before you use it for the first time, you must wash a new wok inside and out with hot water and washing-up liquid. Rub the wok dry, then place a little oil in it and heat it until the oil smokes. Let it cool, wash in hot water, dry and rub a little oil around the inner surface. Many woks are oiled in this way after each use. This is unnecessary in the case of coated or stainless steel woks. Whatever kind of wok you have, follow the manufacturer's instructions for use.

Modern woks

You can buy woks with a flattened base for use on our modern electric stoves; they sit firmly on the hob and make the fullest possible use of the heat. Woks are available in a wide range of different designs and qualities. Some are Teflon coated, to prevent food sticking. Most woks have a diameter of 35–40 cm/14–16 in, although there are smaller ones whose diameter is only about 25 cm/10 in. Even for a small household, however, it is better to buy a large wok. Dishes for just one person are more easily cooked in a large than in a small wok.

You cannot put a wok with a wooden handle in a hot oven. However, wooden handles have the advantage of not getting hot.

• Woks made of aluminium or iron are cheapest, but are seldom sufficiently well made for use on electric hobs.

Accessories

Most woks are supplied with a variety of accessories. All these accessories can also be bought in kitchen utensil shops or in Chinese shops:

• Virtually all woks are supplied with a high-domed lid. Only with such a lid can a wok be used for stewing, braising or steaming.

• The semi-circular wire rack is hung from the edge of the wok. It can be used for steaming, draining deep-fried food or keeping stir-fried food warm.

•The long wooden chopsticks are used for stirring food.

• The chan is the classic Chinese spatula with a rounded edge that makes it most suitable for use with the circular wok.

• The chan fits perfectly into the ladle, so that both utensils can be used to lift food out of the wok.

• The strainer is used to lift deep-fried food out of the fat, or to take large pieces of food out of the sauce.

• The bamboo brush is used to clean the wok.

• Chopsticks for eating with are often supplied with woks.

• A spirit burner or perforated metal stand. Make sure that the spirit burner has a large flame or, even better, several flames, so that it generates sufficient heat.

• A large cleaver is used in Asia both for chopping and cutting. A large, heavy, sharp knife will do just as well.

• Bamboo baskets are useful for steaming. You can even stack several on top of each other. Flameproof plates will serve just as well. Both baskets and plates can be placed on a simple wooden rack (which can usually be bought with the wok) or on an upturned cup.

From top to bottom: Bamboo brush, strainer, chan, ladle, cleaver, chopsticks and bamboo steamer.

Cooking with a wok

You can use a wok for frying, steaming, deep-frying, braising and "normal cooking".

• Stir-frying is the one wok technique that is different from any used in Western cooking. The finely chopped ingredients are cooked for the shortest possible time over a hot flame, with everything being kept constantly moving at speed. It is easier to keep the food moving quickly in the large, circular pan than in a normal frying pan, since nothing falls out.

The rapid movement prevents the ingredients from burning, so you need to use only a small amount of oil. Nevertheless, delicious meals can be prepared in no time. Meat is sealed quickly, for maximum retention of juices and flavour; vegetables remain crunchy and the aromas of the fresh ingredients are retained, together with health-giving vitamins. Important note: the cooking time is so short that all ingredients should be thoroughly prepared before any cooking begins. It is also important to do things in the right order: the ingredients requiring the longest cooking time should be put into the wok first. These include, for example, fibrous vegetables such as carrots. Softer ingredients such as mushrooms or bean sprouts should not be added until later.

First heat the wok without any oil. Then pour in the oil and heat to just below smoking point; only then should you start stir-frying. If you are cooking large quantities of food, it is better to work in stages, otherwise not all the ingredients will come into contact with the hot bottom of the wok. Food in a wok is generally fried very rapidly over a high flame (unless the recipe indicates otherwise).

• Steaming is a healthy cooking method that retains much of the food's natural goodness. It is particularly suitable for tender, fresh ingredients such as fish and seafood or vegetables. Steamed dishes are particularly popular in China.

Pour about 750 ml/1½ pints of water or stock into the wok and bring to the boil. The ingredients are covered and placed inside the wok, without being immersed in the liquid, and are cooked in the steam. The little bamboo steamers that can be bought in Asian shops are very decorative. However, you can also steam food on the metal rack that is supplied with most woks. Otherwise, place a heat-resistant dish or cup in the wok and lay a plate with the food to be cooked on top of it. There are two methods of steaming. For wet steaming, the food to be cooked is placed in a bowl inside the bamboo steamer and cooks in the liquid that accumulates inside the basket. For dry steaming, the food to be cooked is placed directly on the wire rack and cooks in the steam.

• Deep-frying: In Thailand and in other Asian countries, "frying" almost always means "deep-frying", a method of cooking for which the wok is also suitable. Its advantage over a conventional saucepan or frying pan is that the wok's tapering shape means less oil is required, only about 500 ml/ 18 fl oz. The ingredients are seldom fully immersed in oil. The oil is heated and then swirled around the wok so that the inner surface is coated. Single pieces of food are browned individually in the oil and then pushed to one side while the next piece is added to the oil. When everything has been browned, all the ingredients are mixed together and fried until fully cooked, with the cook using a ladle to keep everything constantly on the move. The cooked food can be left on the wire rack to drain, or dried off on kitchen paper.

• Braising means that food is first browned and then cooked in a little added liquid. It is a method that is always used when brief stir-frying is not sufficient to cook food thoroughly, and it can take anything from a few minutes to several hours. It is important to have a closely fitting lid.

A wok can be used to cook familiar food as well as new and exotic dishes. For these foreign dishes, of course, you will need unfamiliar ingredients, and it is precisely these unusual foods that offer variety and the opportunity to make exciting new culinary discoveries. You do not have to buy everything all at once if you want to start cooking Asian food. For your first attempts, the essential ingredients are soy sauce, fresh ginger, garlic and chillies. Many dishes acquire that extra something from the addition of fish sauce, rice vinegar, fresh coriander or a mixture of curry spices; coconut milk is also used frequently and abundantly. You can buy all the other ingredients once the passion for Asian food has gripped you. This list is intended to help you become acquainted with the unfamiliar ingredients. It will make shopping easier and you will discover which ingredients might possibly be substituted. Nowadays you can buy Asian ingredients in the food departments of large stores and in supermarkets. And in all larger towns there are specialist Asian shops where you can really get everything you require. With the exception of fresh ingredients, everything can be kept for a long time. If jars, tins and boxes are tightly sealed and stored in a cool, dark place, the contents will keep for at least a year, and many things will last much longer – unless of course you use them up!

Oil

The oil used for cooking should be neutral in taste and capable of being heated to high temperatures, since it must not burn in a hot wok. Groundnut and soya oil are both very suitable. High-quality, cold-pressed oils are unsuitable, as are butter or margarine. In Indian cooking however, ghee is commonly used for frying. Clarified butter can be used as a substitute. Sesame oil made from roasted sesame seeds has a distinctive nutty flavour and so is used for aromatic purposes only, small quantities being added to cooked dishes.

Stock

Many dishes are cooked in stock. This usually means a light fish or chicken stock. You can of course use stock cubes and water, although home-made stock tastes even better. Put a boiling chicken or 1 kg/2 lbs of fish trimmings into a large pan and cover with cold water. Season with herbs, peppercorns and a bay leaf. Bring to the boil, simmer the chicken for about 1½ hours and the fish for about 20 minutes and then strain. The stock can be prepared in advance and frozen.

Stock

Sauces and pastes

Bean sauces are made from yellow, black or red beans. They may take the form of a viscous liquid or even a paste, and there are various flavours. Sweet bean sauces are made from red soya beans, flour, salt, sugar and water. Salty black bean sauce is made from fermented black beans, water, salt, sugar, soya oil and rice wine. It often contains garlic as well. Yellow bean sauce is also salty. Many dishes can be seasoned with soy sauce as a substitute for salty bean sauces.

Chilli sauce is obtained from various countries and varies widely in strength. The hot or sweetish-hot sauce is used for cooking, particularly in Thailand, but is also often served as a side-dish.

Curry pastes are often used in Thailand and India. In those countries, everybody makes their own pastes from fresh spices and a little water or oil. You can buy curry paste in various colours and flavours. The reddish-brown Panang curry is particularly popular.

Recipe for a hot curry paste:
Briefly fry 1 tablespoon peeled cardamom seeds with 2 tablespoons coriander seeds over a medium heat. Add 1 tablespoon mustard seeds, 2 tablespoons peppercorns, 1 stick cinnamon and 6 cloves and brown quickly. Grind all the ingredients to a fine powder. Peel a walnut-sized piece of ginger and 4 cloves garlic and chop finely. Wash 2 large red and 2 large green chillies and chop finely. Add 2 tablespoons turmeric and grind all the ingredients with a pestle and mortar or purée them in a blender. Add oil until a thick paste is formed. Kept in an airtight container and stored in a dark place, it will keep for several weeks.

Fish sauce gives dishes a slight fish flavour. In small quantities it enhances and brings out the other aromas. There are various kinds, so try them out before you use them. They are all very salty and so should be used sparingly. The lighter kinds are to be preferred, most of them being more aromatic. Soy sauce mixed with a little anchovy paste is a possible substitute.

Oyster sauce

Fish sauce

Curry paste

Chillies, cardamoms

Bean sauce

Garlic

Appetizing ingredients

<u>Hoisin sauce</u> is a hot, slightly sweet sauce made from red beans, sugar, garlic and chilli. It is a popular barbecue sauce in China. Sweet soy sauce may be used instead.

<u>Ketjap</u> is a spicy Indonesian sauce made from soya beans. Ketjap asin is bitter-sweet, while ketjap manis is mild and sweet in flavour.

Soy sauce

Rice vinegar

<u>Oyster sauce</u> gives dishes a mild flavour of the sea. It is thick, very dark and salty and slightly sweet at the same time. It is made from water, sugar, salt, oyster extract and starch. A little anchovy paste can be used as a substitute.

<u>Plum sauce</u> is a thick, reddish-brown, highly aromatic sauce with a fruity, spicy yet sweet flavour. It is made from plums, apricots, garlic, chilli, sugar, salt, vinegar and water and is used in cooking and also as a sauce and dip. There is a recipe for plum sauce on page 35.

<u>Rice vinegar</u> really is made from rice. At 3% proof it is less strong than wine vinegar, which can nevertheless be used as a substitute. When used in small quantities, rice vinegar brings out the flavour of individual dishes.

<u>Rice wine</u> (sake in Japanese) is made from fermented rice; its alcohol content is approximately 18%. It varies widely in quality, with some kinds being used for cooking and others being served warm with meals. A little dry sherry or white port can be used instead.

<u>Sambals</u> are spicy pastes from Indonesia, made from large hot peppers (lombok) or from very hot small chillies (lombok rawit). Sambal oelek is a very hot chilli paste. Sambal brandal is also very hot and is made from roasted peppers, onions, chilli paste, salt and other seasonings. Sambal badjak is somewhat milder than sambal brandal. Sambal manis is sweetish and mildly sharp. It is made from red chillies, onions, sugar, soy sauce, oil, salt, shrimp extract, spices and herbs. Sambal oelek trassie is hot, with an aroma of shrimps. Sambal nasi goreng is milder and is made especially for nasi goreng. Sambal cuka is mildly spicy and contains roasted peanuts. There is a sambal recipe on page 35.

<u>Shrimp paste</u> is made from ground shrimps. The dark, firm paste has a pungent smell but imparts a refined flavour to food. Always mix it first with a little water or soy sauce. Finely chopped anchovies or a little anchovy paste might be used as a substitute.

<u>Soy sauce</u> is popular in all countries of East Asia, although there is a wide variety of different types with more or less distinctive aromas. People in Asia use it in cooking as much as we in Europe use salt, which can almost always be omitted in the preparation of Asian dishes. The commonest types are the dark, salty soy sauces from China (made only from soya beans) and Japan (made from soya and wheat). Light, salty soy sauce is somewhat milder in flavour than the dark variety. It is useful in dishes for which the dark variety would be unsuitable because of its colour. Sweet soy sauce is also dark, but milder and slightly sweet. Molasses are added while it is maturing, hence the sweetish taste. A substitute can be made by adding sugar to salty soy sauce. The Indonesian soy sauces are ketjap asin and ketjap manis.

Herbs and spices

Basil: Thai basil (horapha) looks like our basil but has a faint minty aroma.

Cardamom is a pod with a sweetish aroma, somewhat like eucalyptus. Small quantities impart a mild flavour, while larger amounts taste much hotter. It can be bought as whole pods or as ground seeds.

Chillies are always fiery hot, whether fresh or dried. Small varieties are hotter than the larger ones, and red ones are usually hotter than green ones. Chilli powder is made from ground chillies and other spices. The intensity of the chillies is often alleviated by coconut milk, lemon flavouring or cucumber.

Coriander leaves are used in Asian cooking as we use parsley. Although the soft green leaves are similar in appearance to parsley, the taste is completely different. Use them sparingly: they impart a very intense and unusual flavour. Thai coriander is the mildest. Fresh coriander is usually bought in bunches. Freeze any leftover leaves, so that you always have a supply. There is no substitute. However, it can be easily grown from seeds. See page 48 for details. Coriander seeds have a spicy, rather pungent taste, a little reminiscent of orange peel. They are found in virtually all curries. The seeds give off their best aroma when browned in a frying pan.

Cumin is sometimes confused with caraway, but it tastes completely different. It has a very distinctive, sharply acrid aroma, and should be used sparingly. It is used in most curries. It can be bought as whole seeds or ready ground.

Curry powder is a mixture of many different spices, sometimes as many as thirty. Some of the commonly used ingredients are coriander, pepper, ginger, allspice, paprika, cardamom, cloves, cinnamon, cumin and turmeric. Depending on their composition, the powders may be mild or hot. Sometimes they are mixed with a little oil or water to make a paste. In Indonesia, a curry can be either the cooked dish or the spice.

By the way, you should sample each new curry powder before you use it for the first time and be careful about the amount you use: it may be much hotter than the one you used before.

Two curry recipes:

• Hot curry powder Clean 10 dried red chillies and chop coarsely. In a frying pan, over a moderate heat, gently fry 6 tablespoons coriander seeds, stirring continuously. Quickly brown 2 tablespoons mustard seeds and 4 tablespoons peppercorns with the chillies. Mix everything together with 1 tablespoon ground ginger,

1 teaspoon cloves, 1 stick of cinnamon, and 2 tablespoons ground turmeric. Grind to a fine powder with a pestle and mortar, in a blender or in a pepper mill. Stored in the dark in an airtight container, the powder will keep for several weeks.

• Indonesian garam masala In a dry pan, over a medium heat, gradually brown 1 tablespoon whole cumin seeds, 2 tablespoons coriander seeds, 1 teaspoon cardamom seeds, half a teaspoon white peppercorns, 2 sticks of cinnamon and 1 teaspoon cloves. Take the roasted cardamom seeds out of the pods. Grind everything finely with a pestle and mortar or in a food processor. Add half a grated nutmeg and mix thoroughly. The garam masala will keep for several weeks packed in an airtight container and stored in a dark place.

Djahé is Indonesian for ground ginger (see under Ginger).

Djintan is Malay for cumin (see under Cumin).

Basil

Chillies

Galingale

Five-spice powder is a spice much used by Hindus. It may consist of mustard seeds, cumin, caraway, fenugreek and fennel seeds, while other mixtures contain star anise, allspice or pepper, fennel seeds, cloves and cinnamon.

Galingale is a ginger-like rhizome. It is somewhat milder and sharper than ginger, but is still intensely aromatic. You can buy galingale fresh as a whole stem, or dried, either in slices or ground (when it is known as Laos powder). The whole stem can be stored in the same way as ginger. A little lemon peel can be added to ginger to make an acceptable substitute.

Garlic is used in virtually all Asian dishes. Always use fresh cloves.

Ginger is, like galingale, an aromatic rhizome. It can be bought fresh or dried. You can also buy ground ginger and ginger preserved in a sweet syrup. Depending on the quantity used, it can be either sharply aromatic or hot and pungent. The fresh stem, wrapped in foil, can be kept for at least a week in the refrigerator, and it can also be frozen.

1. *Cardamom* **2.** *Palm sugar*
3. *Sesame seeds* **4.** *Mace* **5.** *Star anise*
6. *Coriander seeds* **7.** *Kerrie djawa*
8. *Szechwan pepper* **9.** *Turmeric root and powder* **10.** *Lemon grass*
11. *Kaffir lime leaves* **12.** *Cumin seeds*
13. *Tamarind*

Kaffir lime leaves are the leaves of a special citrus tree. They have a very sour flavour. Use whole in the same way as bay leaves, or cut out the centre vein and stem, roll up the leaf and cut into the thinnest possible strips. Use as a seasoning or sprinkle over dishes just prior to serving.

Kerrie djawa is a mild, subtly spiced curry powder in the Javanese style. It is made from a mixture of coriander, turmeric, cumin, pepper, cardamom, fenugreek, ginger, fennel, cloves and nutmeg.

Laos is the Malay name for galingale (see under Galingale).

Lemon grass is a thickish, reed-like grass. The hard stems have a powerful lemon-like aroma and flavour. Peel away the dry outer leaves and use only the lower part of the stems. They can be chopped or crushed, and are often soaked as well. Dried lemon grass is available in strips or in powder form.

Mace is a spice made from the dried, orange-brown seed cover of the familiar nutmeg; it is available ground or in strips. Mace has a bitter-sweet aroma, but is more subtle and delicate than nutmeg. Use sparingly.

Monosodium glutamate is often used in Asia as a flavour enhancer. However, the white powder causes headaches and allergic reactions in some people, and for that reason I have stopped using it. It is better, when buying and preparing food, to make sure all ingredients are absolutely fresh and of the best quality, so that everything has sufficient flavour. You can always use a pinch of sugar to enhance the flavour of dishes.

From top to bottom:
Ginger, coriander and garlic

Palm sugar is a dark sugar that can be bought as a paste or in a lump. Before use, dissolve it in a little warm water or warm soy sauce. Brown sugar can be used instead.

Sereh is the Malay name for lemon grass (see Lemon grass).

Sesame has an agreeably pungent flavour and is used in many Asian countries. The whole seeds are as popular as the paste (known as tahini) or the very aromatic sesame oil.

Star anise The decorative, star-shaped pods are the dried fruits of a southern Chinese magnolia tree. It has a pronounced aniseed aroma, but a hot, spicy, slightly sweet flavour. Depending on the intensity of flavour desired, use a single point or a whole pod.

Szechwan pepper is not actually a pepper. The dried red pods come from a Chinese tree. They should be roasted before use, so that their full aroma is released. Black pepper can be used as a substitute.

Tamarind is a bean-like pod, up to 20 cm/8 in in length and cinnamon coloured, the fruit of the Indian tamarind tree. It contains an acidic pulp that is usually sold as a paste and used to add a sour flavour to food. It is often diluted with water prior to use and passed through a sieve. A little lemon juice may be used as a substitute.

Tandoori is an Indian spice mixture containing turmeric, paprika, cardamom, chillies, garlic, coriander, cumin, pepper, saffron, nutmeg, cinnamon and cloves. A special clay oven is also known in India as a tandoor.

Turmeric is, like ginger, a stem. It is not often found fresh in Europe, but is readily available in powder form. It is a bright orange-yellow colour and adds colouring to all curries and many other dishes.

Wasabi is green horseradish. It is popular in Japan and extraordinarily hot. It can be bought as a paste or a powder. Our familiar horseradish can be used instead.

Other typical ingredients

Bamboo shoots are the flavoursome, ivory-coloured shoots of various types of bamboo. Fresh ones are virtually unobtainable in the West, and we have to make do with tinned ones, whether in large chunks or ready sliced. Put any leftover bamboo shoots in a bowl, cover with cold water and store in the refrigerator. With frequent changes of water they will keep for two weeks. You can also freeze them.

Bean sprouts are the shoots of the mung bean, a type of soya bean. They can be eaten raw (after blanching), although the sprouts of the yellow soya bean must be cooked before eating, because they are poisonous when raw. Fresh bean sprouts can now be bought all year round. They are wonderfully crunchy and aromatic. Tinned bean sprouts are soft and lacking in flavour. Fresh bean sprouts can be kept for two or three days in the refrigerator before they begin to go off.

Coconut milk gives a very distinctive aroma to many dishes, and also absorbs some of the heat of chillies. You can buy creamed coconut in block form; it has to be grated and mixed with a little liquid before use. Powdered coconut milk is also available; this also has to be mixed with a little liquid. It is easiest to used tinned coconut milk. Caution: coconut milk can be bought sweetened or unsweetened. The sweetened variety is used only in desserts. You can also pour hot water over fresh or dried grated coconut and leave to stand for 15–30 minutes. Squeeze out all the liquid through a clean tea towel and use as coconut milk.

Edible fungi are both vegetable and flavouring in Asian cookery.
Cloud ears are Chinese morels that are only available here in their dried form. These black fungi have little taste of their own and are often a little leathery. They should be softened in warm water for about 10 minutes before use. At this stage, cut out any little hard "eyes" and chop finely.
Tong koo or shiitake mushrooms can be bought fresh or dried. These dark brown mushrooms are very delicate and aromatic, and bear some resemblance to the cep found in Europe. Soak dried mushrooms (they can be bought whole or, more economically, finely chopped) for 10–12 minutes in warm water before cutting off the tough stems.

Noodles are as popular in Asia as they are in Italy. There are various kinds. Cellophane noodles look transparent, whether raw or cooked. They are made from ground soya beans, mung beans and tapioca root. They hardly need to be boiled; they can be deep-fried or left to soak for a few minutes in warm water and then cooked, or heated up, in a sufficient amount of sauce. Rice noodles are made from rice flour and water and actually taste slightly of rice. When raw, they look transparent like cellophane noodles and turn white when cooked. They can be bought in the form of thin or thick vermicelli or as broad ribbon noodles. You can soak them for a few minutes in warm water and then fry them or cook them in a sauce. Rice noodles can also be deep-fried.
Egg noodles are made of wheat flour. They are sometimes flavoured with shrimp or fish powder. Various kinds are available; all of them have to be cooked in boiling water.

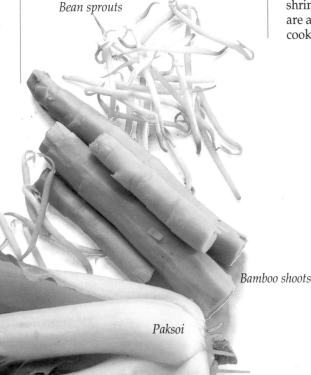

Bean sprouts

Bamboo shoots

Paksoi

Paksoi is a green leafy vegetable, originally from Asia but now grown in Europe. There are many similar leafy vegetables in Asia that are seldom available in Europe, and even then only in specialist Asian shops. One popular example is mustard greens, which has a slightly bitter aroma. Chicory could be used as a substitute.

Rice exists in many varieties in Asia, and is prepared in many different ways. Even Asian shops in this country sell a number of different types. It is usually supposed to be glutinous when cooked (sticky rice), to make it easier to eat with chopsticks. The delicate, aromatic rice known as Basmati can be bought in supermarkets, and various other kinds can be bought in Asian shops. Basmati is known as the "fragrant" rice. It grows on the slopes of the Himalayas and has a distinctive delicate flavour.

Rice papers are transparent circular or wedge-shaped wrappers, made from rice flour and available in various sizes, used to make spring rolls. They must be soaked in cold water before use. Spring onions have long been familiar in the West. In Asia, they are usually much smaller, thinner and milder.

Spring roll skins, made from wheat flour and used to make the crispy starters, can be bought deep-frozen in various sizes. Unused skins can be refrozen. Thin pancakes can be used as a substitute (see page 30).

Tofu is made from soya bean milk. It takes the form of white, milky, custard-like squares and has a low fat content but a lot of valuable protein. It has little flavour of its own and so can be used equally well for sweet or for savoury dishes. However, it always requires a lot of flavouring or seasoning, otherwise it tastes very insipid. You can buy it packaged in virtually every supermarket, health food store or Asian shop.

Won ton wrappers are 10–cm/4–in squares of noodle dough used as the outer envelope for various fillings. They can be bought deep-frozen, and any left-over wrappers can be refrozen.

Shiitake mushrooms

Aromatic rice

Tofu

Won ton wrappers

Rice papers

Prepare properly – Cook in seconds

Food stir-fried in a wok cooks in a flash – provided you have already chopped all the ingredients into slices, cubes or strips of equal size. It is important that everything should be the same size, so that all the food cooks evenly and in the same time. It is especially important that you have really prepared everything thoroughly before you start to cook.

The food cooks so quickly that you will have no time for chopping; in any case, you will not have a hand free while you are stir-frying.

Begin with ingredients that need marinating. While the fish or meat is soaking up the marinade, you can cook the rice or noodles or soak the mushrooms. Only then should you clean and chop the other ingredients and get ready all the spices and utensils you will require. Fresh vegetables should be chopped last of all and then kept well covered until needed.

Some cutting techniques

In Chinese cooking in particular, ingredients are not simply chopped into small pieces but are cut up with great care. The natural flavour of food should arrive on the table unimpaired, everything should be evenly cooked and dishes should also be a pleasure to the eye.

• Slices: cut vegetables, meat (always across the grain) and fish into slices (usually thin slices). Vegetables are commonly sliced at an angle into bite-sized pieces.

• Strips: cut firm vegetables firstly into thick or thin slices and then into matchstick-sized pieces. Leafy vegetables are often cut at an angle into strips 1–2 cm/½–1 in wide.

• Cubes: cut ingredients into thick slices, then into thick sticks and finally into very small cubes.

• Chopping: chop ingredients finely with a cleaver or a large, heavy knife. Mincers are virtually unknown in Asian kitchens, and meat is cut into very small cubes with a cleaver. First cut the meat into thin slices, then into thin sticks and finely into very small cubes.

• Decorative shapes: for quarters, cut vegetables lengthways in four and then cut into slices. For rectangles, cut vegetables into 4–5 cm/1½–2 in pieces, then place the pieces on their end and cut lengthways into thin slices. For half-moons, round vegetables are cut in half lengthways and then cut into thick slices. Even triangles and irregular, wedge-shaped pieces are popular. For chrysanthemums, cut vegetables into 4–5 cm/1½–2 in pieces and then cut a chequered pattern into one end of each piece. Soak in cold water – each piece will open up like a flower. To cut vegetables into flower shapes, cut out four or six wedges lengthways and then cut the stems into slices. Vegetables such as carrots, radishes and cucumbers are often "sharpened to a point", like a pencil.

Delicious meals from the wok

Cooking for guests can be enormous fun – and by serving delicious meals cooked in a wok you will be offering new delights that will beguile all food lovers. You can cook in the wok in the kitchen as usual and bring everything to table on plates and in serving dishes. However, the wok also offers a much more exciting way of entertaining guests. Put the prepared ingredients on the table, together with the wok on a (powerful!) spirit burner. You can then cook a meal before the admiring eyes of your guests. If you want to be even more sociable, why not get everyone to prepare their own little snacks, just as you do at a fondue? You must have a good spirit burner, otherwise the heat will be inadequate. One alternative, though a very expensive one, is to obtain an electric wok, or individual hotplates. The ingredients should include spices and seasonings such as spring onions, garlic and ginger as well as vegetables such as leeks, carrots, peppers, fresh bean sprouts and courgettes. Chop everything finely into equal, bite-sized pieces. You can also add a variety of different types of meat and fish. Select high-quality cuts, such as fillet steak, since the cooking time is too short for less tender cuts. The meat and fish should also of course be chopped into small pieces. To add a particularly sophisticated touch, leave meat or fish to soak for a few hours beforehand in a well-seasoned marinade. You should also serve steamed rice (try Basmati or other fragrant types) or noodles (eg cellophane noodles already soaked in warm water or Chinese egg noodles).

It is also quite important to serve as many different seasonings and sauces as possible. Ginger, garlic, soy sauce, chilli and fish sauce are some typical Asian seasonings. And in super-markets and Chinese shops you can buy a whole range of different spices and seasonings. Try them out. Now the fun can start. Heat the wok and pour in a little oil, not more than 2 or 3 tablespoons. The ingredients with the longest cooking time should go in first, those with the shortest cooking time last. The food in the wok has to be kept constantly on the move, so that everything cooks evenly and nothing burns. Warning: when you put food into the wok, the hot oil might spit! Keep your distance! Most of the recipes will feed four people. For guests, however, it is better to make half the quantity given for each dish and to serve two or three other dishes as well, depending on the number of people present. This is a good idea because cooking times are usually quite short.

Eating with chopsticks

Serving Asian food naturally involves eating with chopsticks as well. However, chopsticks are not used every-where in Asia. Indians, for example, eat with the right hand, while Indonesians use a fork in the left hand and a spoon in the right. The Chinese have been eating with chopsticks since the Shang dynasty (1766–1123 BC), and every small child learns how to use them. It is not difficult: the lower chopstick rests motionless in the hollow between the thumb and index finger. Chunks of food are picked up with the upper chopstick only – you hold it like a pencil and move it with the index and middle fingers and the tip of the thumb.

Desserts for a sweet end to the meal

Sweet desserts are less popular in Asia than in this country, and meals are seldom rounded off with a sweet course. Nevertheless, a sweet dish is often very welcome after a succession of spicy ones. You could, for example, offer guests a colourful fruit salad made from a variety of exotic fruits and perhaps sprinkled with desiccated coconut or marinaded in a coconut liqueur. Ice cream is wonderfully refreshing – you could even try a coconut ice cream or sorbet. Baked bananas, bananas cooked in coconut milk or a light, sweet coconut soup would also make suitable desserts.

Decorating the table

Just one glance at the table should tell your guests they are about to feast on Asian specialities. You can buy bundles of banana leaves in Asian shops; cut place mats out of them. Or try using black foil as a tablecloth and combining it with various shades of red. Just strew the table with a lot of red rose leaves, possibly with grains of rice scattered between them. Other Asian-style decorations such as lacquerwork bowls and plates, stands for chopsticks, fans, Japan paper, paper with Asian characters or rice bags can be bought in Chinese shops or in supermarkets. You could also decorate cardboard with Chinese characters of your own devising – they don't have to be correct!

Another idea for a pretty decoration is to fill a bowl with water and float some lilies or other flowers in it. To give a genuine Asian feel to your table, serve sauces and dips in small bowls, supply matching stands for the chopsticks and provide each guest with a bowl on a small plate for rice and the other dishes.

What to drink

If you would like to serve an aperitif, the best choice would be plum wine, either straight or in a cocktail. For example, combine one part plum wine with two parts pineapple juice and crushed ice. Or mix two parts plum wine with one part sweet vermouth and ice. Garnish the cocktail with an exotic fruit, perhaps a lychee or a piece of pineapple. Mineral water, a light fruit juice or tea are the most suitable drinks to accompany the meal. The delicate, light, unfermented green tea is particularly popular in Asia. To make it, infuse 2 teaspoons of tea in about 5 cups of boiling water for just two minutes. Obviously, if you want the tea to be stronger, leave it to brew for longer. You can also serve cold beer with Asian food. Wine is a bit more of a problem, since it does not go well with many of the heavily spiced dishes. The most suitable choice might be a light, slightly fizzy white wine, for example a young Riesling or a Prosecco. With very hot dishes you could try serving a more robust white wine. One typically Asian drink is rice wine or sake. It is drunk warm, which means that its effects are felt particularly quickly.

And now it really is time to start cooking! To alleviate hunger pangs or to accompany an aperitif, you could simply serve crispy prawn crackers. Or you may like to begin the meal with a more sophisticated appetizer. In Asia, soups are served not before a meal but in the middle or at the end. So before an Asian meal cooked in a wok, serve a light salad or, for an even more authentic touch, spring rolls with well-seasoned sauces. Stuffed won ton wrappers or steamed rolls are other alternatives. The wrappers or skins for these delicacies can be bought, ready for use, in Asian shops. You could also start a meal with pickled vegetables or flat unleavened bread, like Indian chapatis or parathas, and these could also be served as accompaniments to the main dishes. Sophisticated sauces, which the following recipes will show you how to prepare in seconds, are a very special substitute for the usual seasonings of salt and pepper.

Prawn crackers

In Chinese and other Asian shops you can buy glassy-looking, hard crisps known variously as krupuk, krupuk udang or just prawn crackers. These thin discs are made from ground prawns and tapioca starch. They are usually light in colour but there are also coloured prawn crackers. The crackers are deep-fried in hot oil and served as an appetizer, accompanied by one or more dips. They can also be served with dishes cooked in the wok. Important note: fry only a small quantity of crackers at a time. They expand quite a lot and should remain immersed in the oil. Remove the cooked crackers with a skimmer after about 30 seconds and drain thoroughly on kitchen paper.

Spring rolls

In China, they were eaten in earlier times to celebrate the new year. Nowadays, spring rolls are common throughout Asia. They are usually round in shape, but they can also be served as triangular parcels. Important note: always seal the rolls or parcels firmly during preparation so that the filling does not fall out during cooking.

Spring rolls can be made with various kinds of wrappers:
• Wrappers made of dried rice paper are available in various sizes, round or square. They should be soaked one by one for a short while in cold water and then laid on a cloth ready for filling. Rice paper wrappers tear easily. Working with them requires a little practice, so expect some wastage and leave plenty of time until you get the hang of it.
• Deep-frozen wrappers (spring roll pastry) are also available in various sizes and are almost always square. They are extremely easy to use. Leave them to defrost, covered with a damp cloth to prevent them drying out. Count out the number you require and refreeze the remainder.
• Thin, freshly made pancakes, which should not be crispy, otherwise they cannot be shaped. Whisk 250 g/8 oz flour with 550 ml/18 fl oz water, 1 egg and ½ teaspoon salt and leave to stand for an hour. Then fry 8–10 thin pancakes in a little oil in a non-stick frying pan. Stack the cooked pancakes and cover with a kitchen towel.

Spring rolls with chicken filling

Ingredients for 8 rolls:
200 g/7 oz chicken breast fillet
1 leek
1 carrot
1 stick celery
2 shallots
2 tablespoons soy sauce
2 tablespoons vegetable oil
freshly ground white pepper
8 spring roll wrappers
oil for frying

Basic recipe

About 690 kJ/160 kcal per portion

Preparation time: about 1 hour

1. Shred the chicken breast fillets very finely. Trim and wash the vegetables, cut them into very thin strips and mix with the chicken.

2. Peel and finely chop the shallots. Mix with the soy sauce, vegetable oil and pepper, add the chicken and vegetable mixture and leave for about 30 minutes.

3. Heat the wok and stir-fry the chicken and vegetable mixture for about 3 minutes before removing it.

4. Prepare wrappers for the spring rolls by making pancakes, defrosting deep-frozen wrappers or soaking rice paper wrappers.

5. Place some filling on each of the wrappers. Fold the wrapper over the filling, turning the sides in towards the centre. Moisten the edges with water and press firmly together.

6. Heat oil for deep-frying in the wok. Deep-fry the spring rolls in batches for about 5 minutes each until golden brown. Remove and drain on kitchen paper.

■ Serve with soy sauce or another dip.

Unleavened breads

Ingredients for 16 breads:
400 g/13 oz floury potatoes
2 medium onions
1 bunch dill
500 g/1 lb wheatmeal flour
2–3 teaspoons salt
3 tablespoons oil
125 ml/4 fl oz lukewarm water
flour for dusting the work surface
clarified butter for frying

Indian parathas

About 580 kJ/140 kcal per bread

Preparation time: about 1 hour
(+ 1 hour standing time)

1. Wash the potatoes and boil in their
skins for about 20 minutes. Drain,
leave to cool a little, then skin and put
through a sieve or press.

2. Peel and finely chop the onions.
Wash the dill, shake dry and chop
finely.

3. Put the flour in a large bowl and
mix in the salt. Add the potatoes,
onions, dill and oil. Gradually add the
water and knead to a smooth dough.
Cover and leave to stand for an hour.

4. Divide the dough into 16 portions,
dust the work surface with flour and
roll out each portion into very thin flat
cakes.

5. Over a medium flame, heat plenty
of clarified butter in the wok or a large
frying pan and fry the parathas for
2–3 minutes on each side until golden
brown. Drain on kitchen paper.

Top: Prawn crackers
Middle: Spring rolls with
chicken filling
Bottom: Unleavened breads

Deep-fried prawn and coconut parcels

Serves 4:
20 won ton wrappers (deep-frozen)
50 g/2 oz coconut cream (in the block)
2 tablespoons oyster sauce
3 tablespoons light soy sauce
salt
freshly ground pepper
½ teaspoon curry paste
250 g/8 oz peeled prawns

From Thailand

About 1600 kJ/380 kcal per portion

Preparation time: about 1 hour

1. Cover the won ton wrappers and leave to defrost.

2. Finely grate the coconut cream and mix with the oyster sauce, soy sauce, salt, pepper and curry paste.

3. Wash the prawns in cold water, dry thoroughly and chop coarsely or very finely as you prefer. Mix with the coconut cream.

4. Remove the won ton wrappers from the pile and put 1 teaspoon of the prawn mixture on to each one. Gather the wrapper carefully round the filling and press firmly to close.

5. Heat oil for deep-frying in the wok. Deep-fry the parcels in batches for 2–3 minutes until golden brown. Remove and drain thoroughly on kitchen paper.

■ Serve with a sweet-sour chilli sauce or soy sauce with ginger, garlic, chopped chillies and finely chopped kaffir lime leaves.

Left: Steamed chicken and mushroom won tons
Bottom: Deep fried prawn and coconut parcels
Top right: Radish salad
Middle right: Carrot salad

Steamed chicken and mushroom won tons

Serves 4:
12 deep-frozen won ton wrappers
(150 g/5 oz spring roll pastry)
15 g/½ oz dried shiitake mushrooms
½ bunch spring onions
200 g/7 oz chicken breast fillet
1 small tin sweetcorn
(approx. 150 g/5 oz)
1 walnut-sized piece fresh ginger
2 tablespoons soy sauce
1 tablespoon chilli sauce
Freshly ground black pepper
1 pinch sugar
1 teaspoon rice wine (or dry sherry)
1 egg white for coating
1 1/1¾ pints hot water

Sophisticated

About 950 kJ/230 kcal per portion

Preparation time: about 1 hour

1. Cover the won ton wrappers and leave to defrost.

2. Wash the mushrooms in cold water and leave to soak in a little warm water for 10 minutes.

3. Trim and wash the spring onions. Reserve a few of the green ends and chop the rest finely into rings.

4. Wash the chicken under the cold tap, dry and shred finely. Mix with the spring onion rings and drained sweetcorn.

5. Drain the mushrooms, remove the stalks, finely chop the caps and add to the chicken mixture.

6. Peel and finely chop the ginger. Mix with the soy sauce, chilli sauce, pepper, sugar and rice wine or sherry and add to the chicken mixture.

7. Put some filling in the middle of each wrapper. Brush the edges with lightly whipped egg white. Gather the wrapper around the filling and press close to give the shape of a little money bag. Cut the reserved spring onion tops into long, thin strips and use them to "tie" the parcels.

8. Place the parcels in a steamer or on a heat-resistant plate and put the steamer into the wok. Pour the water into the wok from the side, bring to the boil and cover with the lid. Steam the dumplings for about 10 minutes over a moderate heat.

▦ Serve with a soy sauce dip.

Sweet-sour soy sauce Trim and chop 2 small red chillies, peel and crush 3 cloves of garlic. Briefly brown in a pan in 1 teaspoon of oil. Stir in 20 g/¾ oz palm or brown sugar and add 6 tablespoons soy sauce and 3 tablespoons rice vinegar. Sprinkle with finely chopped coriander leaves and leave to cool.

Delicious salads

Radish salad
Peel 500 g/1 lb radishes, cut into wafer-thin slices, salt lightly and leave to sweat for a few minutes. Drain off the liquid. Mix 2 tablespoons white wine vinegar with ¼ teaspoon sambal oelek, salt and black pepper, add 4 tablespoons oil and use to dress the radishes. Sprinkle with a few finely chopped coriander or mint leaves.

Carrot salad
Peel and coarsely grate 1 bunch new carrots. Peel and finely chop 1 walnut-sized piece of ginger and 1 garlic clove. Mix with 4 tablespoons light and 2 tablespoons sweet soy sauce, 3 tablespoons oil, salt and black pepper and use to dress the carrots.

Pickles and preserves

Korean vegetables

Trim and wash 500 g/1 lb Chinese cabbage and cut in half lengthways. Pull apart slightly and sprinkle about 100 g/3½ oz salt evenly between the leaves. Cover and leave to stand for about 2 hours. In the meantime, slice 1 small red pepper in half and cut it into very fine strips. Trim 1 small leek, slit open, wash and chop into very thin rings. Peel 1 small radish, and chop first into thin slices and then into thin strips. Peel and finely chop 2–3 cloves garlic and 50 g/2 oz fresh ginger and mix with 1 tablespoon sugar, white pepper, 2 teaspoons paprika, 125 ml/4 fl oz water and the chopped pepper, leek and radish. Wash the Chinese cabbage thoroughly and leave to drain. Place the seasoned vegetables between the cabbage leaves. Put the Chinese cabbage in a glass jar or stoneware pot, cover with a plate and press firmly with a weight. Keep the cabbage covered in the refrigerator for at least 2 days until it tastes slightly sour. The vegetables will keep well for a month. In Korea they are chopped and served with all hot rice dishes.

Japanese radishes

Peel 250 g/8 oz radishes and cut them into thin slices and then into ½ cm/¼ in strips. Put into two small, well-cleaned jars and sprinkle with 3–4 tablespoons chopped parsley. Boil up 175 ml/6 fl oz water with the same amount of rice vinegar. Add 3 tablespoons light soy sauce, lemon pepper and 1–2 tablespoons grated green or white horseradish. Bring to the boil briefly, then pour into the jars. Seal tightly and leave overnight. If tightly sealed, the radishes will keep in the refrigerator for at least 2 weeks.

Japanese ginger cucumber

Cut 375 g/12 oz cucumber in half lengthways and remove the seeds. Thinly slice each half and put into 2 small, well-cleaned jars. Peel a walnut-sized piece of ginger, chop it very finely and boil up with 175 ml/ 6 fl oz water and the same amount of rice vinegar. Stir in 3 tablespoons light soy sauce, 1 teaspoon pepper and 1–2 tablespoons grated white or green horseradish, bring to the boil again and pour over the cucumber. Seal tightly and leave in the refrigerator overnight. The cucumber will keep tightly sealed in the refrigerator for at least 2 weeks.

Apricot chutney

Chutneys are highly-spiced, sweet-sour pastes with the consistency of thick jam. They come originally from East India and make a tasty accompaniment to meat, fish and other dishes; they can also be added as a delicious seasoning to dishes being cooked. Chutneys can be bought ready-made, but home-made ones taste even better. You can make them from a wide range of different ingredients. They are always based on a fruit (apricots, mangoes) or a vegetable (eg tomatoes), to which are added sugar and vinegar, a wide range of spices and seasonings and often raisins as well. The ingredients are cooked slowly over a low heat until they form a thick paste. Chutney can be served fresh or can be put while still warm into small jars – it will keep for months if tightly sealed. The following recipe for an apricot chutney will produce enough to fill 2 small jars: Heat 2 tablespoons oil in a large shallow pan and fry 500 g/1 lb chopped onion over a low heat for 10 minutes. Add 200 g/7 oz chopped ripe apricots and 5 tablespoons chicken stock. Finely chop 2 red chillies and add to the onions, together with salt, pepper, 5 tablespoons apple vinegar, 65 g/2½ oz sugar and 1 teaspoon ground coriander. Cook, uncovered, over a very low heat for about 1 hour, stirring repeatedly.

Korean vegetables

Japanese radishes

Delicious, easy-to-prepare dips

Miso dip
Trim and wash 1 spring onion and cut it into thin rings. Peel and chop a walnut-sized piece of ginger. Mix the spring onion and ginger with 1 tablespoon miso and 3 tablespoons water (or 4 tablespoons soy sauce), 5 tablespoons soya oil, 125 ml/4 fl oz wine vinegar and 1 tablespoon clear honey.

Chilli sauce
Trim and seed 1 small red and 1 small green chilli and chop into very thin rings. Mix with 3 tablespoons soya oil, 2 teaspoons clear honey, 5 tablespoons soy sauce and 5 tablespoons stock.

Watercress sauce
Wash, dry and shred 125 g/4 oz watercress. Mix together 100 ml/3¾ fl oz red wine vinegar, 6 tablespoons salty soy sauce and 1 tablespoon sweet soy sauce, white pepper, 5 tablespoons soya oil and 3 tablespoons sesame oil and pour over the cress.

Sweet-sour tomato sauce
Press the contents of a 400 g/14 oz tin of tomatoes through a fine sieve and reduce over a high flame to a thick consistency. Then mix in 1 tablespoon sherry, 2 tablespoons apple vinegar, 5 tablespoons soy sauce and 1 tablespoon clear honey. Season with black pepper.

Peanut and cucumber sauce
Trim and chop 4 small red chillies into thin rings. Peel and chop 1 hazelnut-sized piece ginger and 2 cloves garlic. Peel and grate 100 g/3½ oz cucumber. Grind 65 g/2¼ oz roast salted peanuts. Mix with 40 g/1½ oz palm or brown sugar, 3 tablespoons lime juice, 2 tablespoons light soy sauce and 125 ml/4 fl oz water and simmer uncovered over a low heat for 5–10 minutes. Sprinkle with finely chopped coriander leaves and leave to cool.

Red chilli sauce
In a small saucepan, bring to the boil 100 g/3¾ oz sugar, 1 teaspoon salt, 6 tablespoons vinegar, 2 heaped teaspoons sambal oelek and 75 g/3 oz tomato purée, stirring constantly. Mix 1 level teaspoon cornflour and a little water to a smooth paste, add to the sauce and simmer until the sauce thickens, stirring constantly. Leave to cool.

Sambal
Slit the skins of 500 g/1 lb tomatoes, pour boiling water over them, peel, remove the seeds and dice finely. Trim and wash 1 red pepper and 3 small red chillies and chop finely. Peel 1 small onion and 2 cloves garlic, chop finely and fry in 2 tablespoons oil in the wok until transparent. Add the pepper and chilli, mix everything together and cook for a few minutes over a low heat, stirring constantly. Season with 2 teaspoons ground galingale, 2 teaspoons ground coriander and 1 tablespoon tamarind paste. Stir in the tomatoes, cover and cook over a moderate heat for about 30 minutes. Leave the sauce to cool.

Plum sauce
Wash 500 g/1 lb plums, cut in half and remove the stones. Place the plums in a large pan. Peel 1 large onion, chop and add to the pan. Peel and chop 25 g/1 oz ginger and mix with 65 g/2¼ oz sugar, 125 ml/4 fl oz fruit vinegar, ⅛–1 teaspoon ground coriander and ½–1 teaspoon sambal oelek. Bring to the boil, stirring constantly, then simmer uncovered over a very low heat, stirring frequently, for about 30 minutes. Leave to cool.

Red chilli sauce

Peanut and cucumber sauce

Chilli sauce

Watercress sauce

Plum sauce

Sambal

Meat and poultry

Meat and poultry are usually the centrepiece of any special meal, and there is no reason why that should not be the case with meals cooked in a wok. However, you will have to forego a large Sunday roast or a whole bird. Otherwise, there is no limit on the range of dishes that can be prepared. Choose between classic recipes and new ones, between pork, succulent beef, tasty lamb or tender chicken. Even reasonably priced minced meat can be given a new lease of life in the wok. Whatever you choose to serve, you will be amazed how little meat you need to use. So you will be right up-to-date with the latest ideas on healthy eating!

Beef with baby corn

Serves 4:
1 bunch spring onions
500 g/1 lb fillet of beef
2 teaspoons five-spice powder
6 tablespoons fish sauce
4 tablespoons sweet bean sauce
freshly ground white pepper
100 ml/3½ fl oz water
1 teaspoon cornflour
3 tablespoons oil
400 g/13 oz baby corn (canned or fresh)
fresh basil (about 1 tablespoon finely chopped leaves, plus some whole leaves for garnish)

For special occasions

About 1400 kJ/330 kcal per portion

Preparation time: about 30 minutes

1. Trim and wash the spring onions and cut at a very sharp angle into thin rings.

2. Wash and dry the beef fillet and cut first into thin slices and then into bite-sized pieces. Sprinkle with the five-spice powder.

3. Mix the fish sauce with the bean sauce, pepper, water and cornflour.

4. Heat the wok and then pour in the oil and heat. Stir-fry the spring onions for about 2 minutes, and then push them to the edge.

5. Brown the beef in the middle of the wok for about 1 minute. As it browns, push the pieces of meat to the side of the wok. When all the meat has browned, mix it with the spring onions.

6. Stir the sauce once again (the cornflour will have settled to the bottom) and pour into the wok. Add the drained baby corn and stir-fry all the ingredients for a further 2–3 minutes. Finally stir in the chopped basil. Garnish with whole basil leaves and serve.

■ Serve with rice noodles, broad ribbon noodles or rice. A chilli pepper cut to form a "flower" makes an attractive decoration.

Pork with fish sauce

Serves 4:
3–4 red chillies
4 cloves garlic
6 tablespoons sweet soy sauce
4 teaspoons lemon juice
8 tablespoons fish sauce
1 teaspoon freshly ground white pepper
150 ml/¼ pint stock
1½ teaspoons cornflour
500 g/1 lb pork escalope or fillet
2 green peppers
2 yellow peppers
4 tablespoons oil

Quite simple

About 1300 kJ/310 kcal per portion

Preparation time: about 50 minutes

1. Trim, wash and seed the chillies, then chop finely. Peel the garlic and cut into very thin strips. Mix both with soy sauce, lemon juice, fish sauce, pepper, stock and cornflour, and leave to stand for about 30 minutes.

2. Wash and dry the pork. Cut into thin slices and then into bite-sized squares. Put into the marinade and mix thoroughly.

3. Cut the peppers in half, trim and wash and cut into thin diamond shapes.

4. Heat the wok, then pour in the oil and heat. Stir-fry the peppers for about 4 minutes and push to the edge.

5. Remove the meat from the marinade, drain and brown for about 2 minutes in the middle of the wok, pushing the browned meat to the edge.

6. Pour the marinade into the wok, mix all the ingredients together and briefly stir-fry.

■ Serve with rice or cellophane noodles.

Variation
Soak 75 g/3 oz cellophane noodles in hot water, chop into small pieces and mix in at the end.

Steamed chicken

Serves 4:
500 g/1 lb chicken breast fillet
2 cloves garlic
1 teaspoon sambal oelek
3 tablespoons soy sauce
1 tablespoon mango chutney
1 very small Chinese cabbage (about 250 g/½ lb)
about 900 ml/1¾ pints boiling water
salt andfreshly ground black pepper
2 tablespoons roast peanuts
a few sprigs fresh coriander

Low in calories

About 710 kJ/170 kcal per portion

Preparation time: about 45 minutes
(+ 1–2 hours marinating time)

1. Wash the chicken breast fillets under the cold tap, dry and cut into thin strips.

2. Peel the garlic, chop very finely and mix with the sambal oelek, soy sauce and chutney. Add the meat, mix thoroughly, cover and leave to marinate in the refrigerator for 1–2 hours.

3. Trim and wash the Chinese cabbage and remove the leaves from the stalk. Place the leaves in a steamer or on a heat-resistant plate and season with salt and pepper. Place the chicken meat on the bed of leaves.

4. Place the steamer or plate in the wok and pour in the water from the side. Put the lid tightly on the wok and steam over a moderate heat for about 12 minutes. It may be necessary to turn the chicken meat carefully as it steams, so that it cooks evenly. (If the pieces are well spread out they will not need turning.)

5. Chop the peanuts and sprinkle with the coriander leaves over the cooked meat. Serve hot.

▨ Serve with rice and a vegetable.

Chicken with mangetout

Serves 4:
500 g/1 lb chicken breast fillet
65 g/2¾ oz fresh galingale (or
2 teaspoons dried galingale;
ginger can be used as a substitute)
2 cloves garlic
4 tablespoons oil
¼–½ teaspoon sambal oelek
5 tablespoons light soy sauce
freshly ground black pepper
300 g/10 oz mangetout
150 ml/½ pint chicken stock
½ teaspoon cornflour
salt

Low in calories

About 960 kJ/230 kcal per portion

Preparation time: about 30 minutes
(+ 3–4 hours marinating time)

1. Rinse the chicken breast fillets under the cold tap, dry and shred.

2. Peel the galingale and garlic and chop very finely. Mix with the oil, sambal oelek, soy sauce and pepper. Add the meat, mix thoroughly, cover and leave in the refrigerator for 3–4 hours.

3. Trim and wash the mangetout and cut crossways into halves or thirds. Mix the stock and cornflour to a smooth paste.

4. Heat the wok. Add the meat and the marinade and brown quickly for just 30 seconds. Push the meat to the edge as it browns.

5. When all the meat is browned, put the mangetout and the thickened stock into the wok and stir-fry everything for a further 5–6 minutes. Season with salt and pepper before serving.

■ Serve with aromatic or other boiled rice.

Spicy beef with bean sauce

The fried meat can easily be pushed to the side of the wok with the help of the chan.

Serves 4:
For the meat:
2 tablespoons cornflour
1 small egg
½ teaspoon freshly ground black pepper
½ teaspoon sugar
5 tablespoons water
3 tablespoons soy sauce
4 red chillies
500 g/1 lb beef fillet
6 tablespoons oil
1 bunch spring onions
2 cloves garlic
For the bean sauce:
2 tablespoons sweet bean sauce
2 tablespoons rice wine
2 tablespoons tomato ketchup
1 teaspoon freshly ground black pepper
3 tablespoons sugar
2 tablespoons soy sauce
125 ml/4 fl oz chicken broth

From China

About 1400 kJ/330 kcal per portion

Preparation time: about 50 minutes

1. Prepare the marinade for the meat by mixing the cornflour with the egg, pepper, sugar, water and soy sauce; leave to stand for 20 minutes.

2. In the meantime, trim, wash and seed the chillies and chop finely. Wash the beef under the cold tap, dry on kitchen paper and shred coarsely.

3. Stir the marinade again, then add 4 tablespoons oil, the chillies and the meat and mix thoroughly.

4. Trim and wash the spring onions and cut into pieces. Peel the garlic and chop finely.

5. Mix together the ingredients for the bean sauce.

6. Heat the wok and then pour in the remaining 2 tablespoons oil and heat. Remove the meat from the marinade, drain and brown quickly in the wok, pushing it to the edge as it browns.

7. Stir-fry the spring onions and garlic in the middle of the wok for 1–2 minutes.

8. Add the meat marinade and the bean sauce, mix everything thoroughly and stir-fry for another minute or so.

■ Serve with rice or Chinese egg noodles.

Variation: Pork with bean sauce
Prepare double the quantity of marinade. Season half of it with oyster or fish sauce and plenty of fresh ginger instead of the chillies. Add pork fillet, cut into small pieces, to this marinade and then cook the meat with vegetables and soy sauce. Use the other half of the marinade for (a correspondingly smaller amount of) beef.

Stir-fried spare ribs

Serves 2:
1 walnut-sized piece fresh ginger
1 clove garlic
2 tablespoons soy sauce
1 tablespoon paprika
½ teaspoon sugar
freshly ground black pepper
1 tablespoon roasted sesame seeds
1 tablespoon sesame oil
500 g/1 lb pork spare ribs (cut into short pieces)
15 g/½ oz tong koo mushrooms
1 small green and 1 small red pepper
3 chillies
2 spring onions
2 tablespoons soya oil
125 ml/4 fl oz water
25 g/1 oz pine kernels
salt

From Korea

About 1000 kJ/240 kcal per portion

Preparation time: about 1½ hours
(+ at least 1 hour marinating time)

1. Peel the ginger and garlic and chop very finely. Mix with the soy sauce, paprika, sugar, pepper, sesame seeds and sesame oil.

2. Chop the spare ribs into individual ribs, and if necessary chop each one into smaller pieces. Rinse under the cold tap and dry. Cover with the marinade and leave in the refrigerator for at least 1 hour.

3. In the meantime, soak the mushrooms in a little warm water. Cut the peppers in half, take out the core, wash and cut into thin strips.

4. Trim and wash the chillies and chop finely. Trim and wash the spring onions and cut at an angle into thin strips.

5. Heat the wok, then pour in the soya oil and heat. Brown the spare ribs, stirring continuously. Pour on the water and simmer uncovered over a low heat for about 30 minutes until the water has almost completely evaporated. Stir several times.

6. Add the mushrooms, together with the water, the vegetables and pine kernels and season with salt and pepper. Simmer, covered, over a low heat for a further 20 minutes.

■ Serve with rice and vegetables or savoury rice.

Serving tip
For 4 people, do not increase the quantities since it is difficult to cook larger quantities in a wok. It would be preferable to prepare a second, different dish (a vegetable dish, for example) and serve the two together.

Pork with bamboo shoots

Serves 4:
For the marinade:
1 small egg
½ tablespoon cornflour
2 tablespoons water
3 tablespoons soy sauce
1 teaspoon freshly ground black pepper
½ teaspoon sugar
In addition:
1 walnut-sized piece fresh ginger
3 cloves garlic
500 g/1 lb pork fillet
200 g/7 oz tinned bamboo shoots
300 g/10 oz fresh beansprouts
1 tablespoon black bean paste
100 ml/3½ fl oz chicken stock
3 tablespoons oil

From China

About 1000 kJ/240 kcal per portion

Preparation time: about 1 hour

1. Whisk the ingredients for the marinade to a smooth consistency and leave to stand for about 30 minutes.

2. In the meantime, peel the ginger and garlic and chop very finely.

3. Wash the pork fillet under the cold tap and dry. Then cut into thin slices and again into broad strips.

4. Add the ginger and the garlic to the marinade and pour over the meat.

5. Cut the bamboo shoots into 1 cm/½ in cubes. Rinse the beansprouts in a sieve and drain thoroughly.

6. Mix the bean paste with the chicken stock.

7. Heat the wok, pour in the oil and heat. Brown the meat for about 3 minutes, stirring constantly, pushing the meat to the edge as it browns.

8. Add the bamboo shoots and beansprouts and stir-fry in the middle of the wok for about 1 minute.

9. Add the bean sauce and the remaining marinade, mix all the ingredients thoroughly and stir-fry for a further 1–2 minutes.

■ Serve with rice or Chinese egg noodles.

Panang duck

Serves 4:
3 duck breast fillets (about 750 g/
1½ lbs)
3 tablespoons sweet soy sauce
3 tablespoons oyster sauce
2 cloves garlic
5 tablespoons oil
10–12 kaffir lime leaves
400 ml/14 fl oz coconut milk
4–5 teaspoons Panang curry paste
5 tablespoons fish sauce

From Thailand

About 1900 kJ/450 kcal per portion

Preparation time: about 40 minutes
(+ 5 hours marinating time)

1. Rinse the duck breast fillets under
the cold tap and dry. Make several
diagonal incisions in the layer of fat,
without cutting into the flesh.

2. Mix the soy sauce with the oyster
sauce. Peel and crush the garlic and
add to the sauce. Pour the liquid over
the duck meat, cover and marinate in
the refrigerator for about 5 hours.

3. Heat the oil in the wok. Fry each
duck breast fillet separately over a
moderate heat, skin side down first of
all, then on the other side, for a total of
about 6 minutes, until they are no

longer very bloody. Take the meat out,
leave to cool for a short time, then cut
into thin slices.

4. Cut the stems out of the kaffir lime
leaves, roll them up and cut into very
thin strips.

5. Mix the coconut milk with the curry
paste and fish sauce.

6. Pour the oil out of the wok. Pour in
the coconut mixture and stir-fry for
about 2 minutes. Add the strips of
duck meat and heat through for about
½ minute. Serve the curry sprinkled
with the kaffir lime leaves.

■ Thai aromatic rice is a must with
this dish.

Sweet and sour duck

Serves 4:
4 duck breast fillets (about 1 kg/2 lbs)
salt and freshly ground white pepper
4 tablespoons rice wine
2 onions
2 cloves garlic
4 sticks celery
4 rings fresh pineapple
300 g/10 oz fresh lychees
2 tablespoons tomato ketchup
4 tablespoons rice vinegar
100 ml/3½ fl oz water
2 teaspoons sugar
4–5 teaspoons cornflour
2 tablespoons oil
4 tablespoons light soy sauce
a little chilli sauce or Tabasco

For special occasions

About 3150 kJ/750 kcal per portion

Preparation time: about 1 hour

1. Trim the skin and fat from the meat, rinse, dry and chop into bite-sized pieces. Rub with salt and pepper, sprinkle with the rice wine and leave to marinate for about 10 minutes.

2. Peel and chop the onions and garlic. Wash the celery and dice finely. Peel and dice the pineapple. Peel and stone the lychees.

3. Mix the ketchup with the vinegar, water, sugar and cornflour.

4. Heat the wok, then pour in the oil and heat. Quickly brown the duck meat and sprinkle with the soy sauce. Remove the browned meat from the wok.

5. Stir-fry the onions, garlic and celery for about 2 minutes. Stir the marinade, pour into the wok and bring to the boil.

6. Add the pineapple, lychees and duck meat, stir-fry briefly to heat the fruit through. Season to taste with chilli sauce or Tabasco.

■ Serve with aromatic rice, a sweet and sour or hot sauce and a vegetable dish.

Pork with mussels

The hot chilli seeds can be removed with a pointed knife or simply washed away.

Serves 4:
1 handful fresh coriander leaves
5–6 cloves garlic
2 fresh red chillies
some grated lemon rind
freshly ground black pepper
125 ml/4 fl oz rich chicken stock
125 ml/4 fl oz dry white wine
4 tablespoons olive oil
500 g/1 lb pork loin
400–500 g/13 oz–1 lb cockles or
mussels (fresh or frozen)

From Portugal

About 1500 kJ/360 kcal per portion

Preparation time: about 40 minutes
(+ 4–5 hours marinating time)

1. Pick over the coriander, and if necessary wash and dry it. Chop up a good half of it; cover the rest and put in the refrigerator.

2. Peel and crush the garlic. Trim the chillies, wash out the seeds and chop finely. Mix the garlic with the chopped coriander, chillies, lemon peel, pepper, stock, wine and 3 tablespoons oil.

3. Rinse the pork under the cold tap, dry and cut into 1–2 cm/½–1 in cubes, carefully removing any sinews and fat. Put the meat into the marinade, cover and leave in the fridge for at least 4 hours.

4. Thoroughly wash the mussels, remove the beards and discard any open or damaged ones.

5. Heat the wok, pour in the remaining olive oil and heat to a moderate temperature. Drain the meat, reserving the marinade. Brown the meat in the wok for about 2 minutes and then remove.

6. Put the coriander marinade and mussels into the wok, cover with the lid and cook the mussels over a moderate heat for 5 – 8 minutes until they have opened. Discard any mussels that remain closed.

7. Put the meat back into the wok and cook, uncovered, for a further 4 minutes. Season to taste and serve sprinkled with the remaining coriander leaves.

■ Serve with beans or broccoli and rice or fried potatoes.

The original dish
This is a Portuguese speciality. It is not cooked in a wok in its country of origin, but can be prepared most successfully in this deep pan.

Growing coriander yourself
Fresh coriander can be difficult to obtain. If you are using dried leaves, leave them to soak for a little while in hot stock prior to use. However, you can easily grow coriander yourself in 2–3 weeks. Put some coriander seeds in a flower pot, cover with a layer of earth and keep moist.
Fresh coriander also freezes very successfully, so it is easy to lay in a supply.

Minced meat with peanuts

Serves 4:
500 g/1 lb carrots
3 tablespoons oil
500 g/1 lb mixed minced meat
2 cloves garlic
125 ml/4 fl oz meat stock
salt
freshly ground black pepper
1 teaspoon ground cumin
75–100 g/3–3½ oz roasted salt peanuts
(depending on taste)

Economical

About 2300 kJ/550 kcal per portion

Preparation time: about 30 minutes

1. Wash and peel the carrots. Cut at an angle into thin slices.

2. Heat the wok, pour in the oil and heat. Add the carrots and stir-fry for about 2 minutes, then push to the edge of the wok.

3. Stir-fry the minced meat in the middle of the wok until it becomes crumbly.

4. When all the meat is browned, mix with the carrots. Peel and crush the garlic. Mix it with the meat, pour on the stock and season with salt, pepper and cumin. Cook over a moderate heat for a further 10 minutes, stirring constantly.

5. Taste the meat and add further seasoning if desired. Coarsely chop the peanuts and mix with the meat, reserving a few to sprinkle over it.

■ Serve with boiled or mashed potatoes.

Fried minced meat with vegetables

Serves 4:
4 onions
4 cloves garlic
4 tablespoons oil
500 g/1 lb mixed minced meat
500–625 g/1–1½ lbs mixed,
unseasoned deep-frozen vegetables
250 ml/8 fl oz vegetable stock
4 tablespoons soy sauce
4 tablespoons dry sherry
salt
freshly ground black pepper

Quick to prepare

About 2500 kJ/600 kcal per portion

Preparation time: about 30 minutes

1. Peel the onions and garlic. Chop the onions finely. Crush the garlic.

2. Heat the wok, pour in the oil and heat. Stir-fry the onions and garlic for about 1 minute. Gradually add the minced meat and stir-fry for about 3 minutes. As it browns, push the meat to the edge of the wok.

3. When all the meat is browned, add the vegetables to the wok. Mix thoroughly with the meat, then add the vegetable stock, soy sauce, sherry, salt and pepper.

4. Cook all the ingredients for a further 8 minutes, stirring constantly. Season to taste with salt and pepper.

■ Serve with granary bread or potatoes and a mixed salad.

Turkey in Gorgonzola sauce

Serves 4:
500 g/1 lb turkey breast fillet
3 red salad onions
1 endive
200 g/7 oz Gorgonzola
2 tablespoons oil
200 g/7 oz single cream
3–4 tablespoons dry sherry
(according to taste)
freshly ground black pepper
salt
20 g/¾ oz chopped walnuts

Quick to prepare

About 2300 kJ/550 kcal per portion

Preparation time: about 30 minutes

1. Rinse the turkey meat under the cold tap, dry and cut into thin slices and then into bite-sized pieces.

2. Peel the onions and cut into thin strips.

3. Trim and wash the endive, dry thoroughly and then cut into strips about 2 cm/1 in across.

4. Cut the rind, if any, off the Gorgonzola, then chop into small cubes or mash with a fork.

5. Heat the wok, then pour in the oil and heat. Stir-fry the turkey meat over a high heat for about 2 minutes. Remove from the wok.

6. Brown the onions in the wok. Pour in the cream, melt the Gorgonzola in it and heat the sauce through.

7. Add the strips of endive, then the turkey meat. Mix everything together and season to taste with the sherry, pepper and salt. Heat everything through for 1–2 minutes, stirring constantly. Serve sprinkled with the chopped walnuts.

Serve with ribbon noodles.

Pork in parsley and cream sauce

Serves 4:
500 g/1 lb pork cutlet
2 medium-sized onions
500 g/1 lb courgettes
300 g/10 oz mushrooms
2 bunches parsley
3 tablespoons oil
250 g/8 oz double cream
200 ml/7 fl oz dry white wine
salt
freshly ground black pepper

For special occasions

About 2500 kJ/600 kcal per portion

Preparation time: about 40 minutes

1. Rinse the pork escalope under the cold tap, dry and cut into bite-sized pieces. Peel the onions and chop finely.

2. Wash the courgettes and slice thinly; halve or quarter any large slices.

3. Wash, trim and slice the mushrooms.

4. Wash the parsley, shake dry and chop finely, discarding any coarse stems.

5. Heat the wok, pour in the oil and heat. Stir-fry the pork for 2–3 minutes, pushing the meat to the edge of the wok as it browns. Add the chopped onions towards the end of the cooking time.

6. Add the courgettes and mushrooms, mix everything together and stir-fry for a further 6 minutes.

7. Stir in the parsley, double cream and wine, season with salt and pepper, mix together and heat through for 3 minutes.

▨ Serve with macaroni or another kind of pasta.

Stir-fried turkey with chard

Serves 4:
500 g/1 lb turkey breast fillet
white of 1 large egg
3 teaspoons cornflour
5 tablespoons ketjap manis
4 teaspoons shrimp paste
freshly ground black pepper
500 g/1 lb chard
3 tablespoons oil
150 ml/¼ pint chicken stock or water
salt

Low in calories

About 1000 kJ/240 kcal per portion

Preparation time: about 40 minutes
(+ 4–5 hours marinating time)

1. Rinse the turkey meat under the cold tap, dry, then cut into thin slices and finally into small pieces.

2. Whisk the egg white with the cornflour, ketjap manis, shrimp paste and pepper. Add the meat, cover and marinade in the refrigerator for 4–5 hours (or overnight).

3. Trim and wash the chard. Cut the stems diagonally into thin slices and the leaves into strips approximately 1 cm/½ in across.

4. Heat the wok, then pour in the oil and heat. Stir-fry the chard stems for 3–4 minutes, then push to the edge.

5. Drain the turkey meat, reserving the marinade. Stir-fry the meat in the middle of the wok for 1–2 minutes. As it browns, push the meat to the edge of the wok.

6. When all the meat is browned, add the chard leaves to the wok and pour in the marinade and stock or water. Mix everything together and stir-fry for a further 4 minutes. Season to taste with salt and pepper.

■ Serve with fried potatoes or rice.

Tip
Instead of chard, you can use spinach, paksoi or any other leafy green vegetable.

Turkey with coconut and cashews

Serves 4:
500 g/1 lb turkey breast fillet
4 tablespoons ketjap asin
3 teaspoons lemon grass powder
(or grated lemon peel)
2 large cloves garlic
2 fresh red chillies
1 bunch spring onions
100 g/3½ oz creamed coconut (in block)
100 g/3½ oz cashew nuts
3 tablespoons oil
200 ml/7 fl oz chicken stock
salt
freshly ground white pepper

Elegant

About 2700 kJ/640 kcal per portion

Preparation time: approximately 50 minutes

1. Rinse the turkey meat under the cold tap, dry and shred coarsely. Mix with the ketjap asin and lemon grass powder or lemon peel.

2. Peel the garlic, trim and wash the chillies and chop both finely.

3. Trim and wash the spring onions. Cut into 5 cm/2 in pieces and then lengthwise into thin strips.

4. Grate the creamed coconut finely.

5. Heat the wok. Stir-fry the cashew nuts until golden brown, and then remove from the wok.

6. Heat the oil in the wok and stir-fry the turkey meat over a high heat for about 1 minute; as it browns, push the meat to the edge of the wok.

7. When all the meat is browned and pushed to the edge, stir-fry the garlic and chilli mixture and then the spring onions in the middle of the wok.

8. Add the grated creamed coconut, pour in the chicken stock, mix all ingredients thoroughly and stir-fry for a further 3–4 minutes. Season to taste with salt and pepper. Sprinkle with the cashew nuts.

■ Serve with rice.

Pork with ginger

Serves 4:
7 tablespoons fish sauce
2 teaspoons sugar
1 tablespoon lemon grass powder
(or lemon juice and grated lemon
rind)
625 g/1½ lb pork escalope
200 g/7 oz fresh ginger
3 medium-sized onions
4 tablespoons oil

From Cambodia

About 1600 kJ/380 kcal per portion

Preparation time: about 40 minutes

1. Mix the fish sauce with the sugar
and lemon grass powder or lemon
peel. Wash the pork escalope, dry,
shred coarsely and mix with the
marinade.

2. Peel the ginger and cut into wafer-
thin slices. Peel the onions, cut into
quarters and then into thin slices.

3. Heat the wok, pour in the oil and
heat. Stir-fry the chopped ginger and
onions, then push to the edge of the
wok.

4. Stir-fry the pork over a high heat in
the middle of the wok; push to the
edge when browned. Finally, mix all
the ingredients and the marinade in
the wok and stir-fry for a further
2 minutes.

■ Serve with rice and salad or a
vegetable dish.

Stir-fried beef with peppers and lemon grass

Serves 4:
5 stalks lemon grass
3–4 cloves garlic
150 g/5 oz shallots
500 g/1 lb beef fillet
2 large red peppers
2 tablespoons oil
5 tablespoons fish sauce
1 teaspoon turmeric
1 teaspoon sugar
freshly ground pepper

From Cambodia

About 960 kJ/230 kcal per portion

Soaking time: 4–5 hours

Preparation time: about 30 minutes

1. Wash the lemon grass. Cut off the hard knots at the end, cut the thick parts of the stems into thin slices and soak in lukewarm water for 4–5 hours.

2. Peel and finely chop the garlic and shallots. Mix with the drained lemon grass.

3. Shred the beef fillet finely and mix with the garlic-onion mixture.

4. Cut the peppers in half, trim, wash and slice thinly.

5. Heat the wok, pour in the oil and heat. Stir-fry the pepper for 2 minutes, then push to the edge.

6. Gradually put the meat in the middle of the wok and stir-fry over a high heat for about 2 minutes. Add the fish sauce, turmeric, sugar and pepper, mix all the ingredients together and cook for a further
2 minutes.

■ Serve with steamed rice.

Variation
If you like, you can add 1 tablespoon ground peanuts before serving.

Fried chicken with almonds

The best way of removing blanched almonds from their skins is to squeeze them between the thumb and forefinger.

Serves 4:
12 dried tong koo mushrooms
(about 20 g/¾ oz)
500 g/1 lb chicken breast fillet
4 tablespoons light soy sauce
4 tablespoons rice wine
white of 1 large egg
salt
freshly ground black pepper
150 g/5 oz almonds
1 large bunch spring onions
1 walnut-sized piece ginger
3 teaspoons cornflour

Elegant

About 1900 kJ/450 kcal per portion

Preparation time: about 1 hour

1. Soak the tong koo mushrooms in 125 ml/4 fl oz warm water.

2. Rinse the chicken breast fillets under the cold tap, dry and chop into bite-sized pieces.

3. Mix the soy sauce with the rice wine, egg white, salt, pepper and 2 teaspoons oil, add the meat and marinade in a cool place for 15–20 minutes.

4. In the meantime, blanch the almonds in boiling water for 1–2 minutes. Drain, rinse in cold water and peel. Dry the almonds.

5. Trim and wash the spring onions. Slice lengthways into halves or quarters, then dice. Peel the ginger and chop finely.

6. Drain the mushrooms and put the water to one side. Slice the mushrooms in half and remove the stalks.

7. Heat the wok, pour in 2 tablespoons oil and heat. Stir-fry the almonds until golden yellow, remove from the wok, drain and put aside.

8. Take the chicken meat from the marinade and drain thoroughly. Keep the marinade.

9. Put the meat into the wok piece by piece and stir-fry for about 1 minute. Push the meat to the edge of the wok as it browns, or remove and put on a plate.

10. Pour the remaining oil into the wok. Stir-fry the spring onions and ginger for about 2 minutes. Mix in the mushrooms.

11. Blend the mushroom water and marinade with the cornflour and pour into the wok. Bring briefly to the boil. Mix in the chicken meat and almonds, season to taste and serve immediately.

■ Serve with rice and a spicy sauce, and perhaps also a vegetable dish.

Creole chicken

Serves 4:
1 large oven-ready chicken
(about 1.5 kg/3¾ lbs)
2 onions
6 cloves garlic
3 cm/1½ in piece ginger
750 g/1½ lbs tomatoes
3 tablespoons oil
1 tablespoon curry powder
1 small packet ground saffron
1–2 teaspoons dried thyme
salt
freshly ground black pepper
200 ml/7 fl oz chicken stock
1 tablespoon freshly chopped parsley

Elegant

About 1800 kJ/430 kcal per portion

Preparation time: about 1¾ hours

1. Wash and dry the chicken, skin and chop into small pieces.

2. Peel the onion, garlic and ginger and chop finely.

3. Make diagonal incisions in the tomatoes, put briefly into boiling water, remove and skin. Chop into small pieces.

4. Heat the wok, pour in the oil and heat. Stir-fry the chicken pieces over a high heat until brown and then remove from the wok.

5. When all the chicken pieces have been browned, stir-fry the onions in the wok until transparent. Add the garlic and ginger and stir-fry briefly with the chicken.

6. Add the curry, saffron, thyme, salt and pepper and mix together, then pour in the stock and add the tomatoes. Put the chicken pieces back into the wok and mix thoroughly with the other ingredients. Put the lid on the wok and braise the chicken over a moderate heat for about 30 minutes, stirring occasionally.

7. Season the sauce and leave to cook a little longer if necessary. Sprinkle with the parsley and serve.

▓ Serve with rice. For a special occasion, serve with wild rice.

Chicken curry with coconut milk

Serves 4:
2 teaspoons coriander seeds
2 teaspoons cumin seeds
4 shallots
4 cloves garlic
3 cm/1½ in piece galingale or ginger
6–8 fresh red chillies
4 stalks lemon grass (or some grated lemon peel)
¾ teaspoon freshly grated nutmeg
2 teaspoons shrimp paste
¾ teaspoon freshly ground black pepper
salt
6 tablespoons oil
500 g/1 lb chicken breast fillet
325 g/11 oz bean sprouts
350 ml/12 fl oz coconut milk
fresh coriander leaves

From Thailand

About 1200 kJ/290 kcal per person

Preparation time: about 1 hour

1. Brown the coriander and cumin seeds in the wok over a low heat without oil. Put in the food blender.

2. Peel the shallots, garlic and galingale or ginger. Trim and seed the chillies. Trim the lemon grass and slice thinly. Put in the blender with the nutmeg, shrimp paste, pepper and salt and add 4 tablespoons oil. Blend everything to a paste.

3. Rinse the chicken breast fillets under the cold tap, drain thoroughly and shred coarsely. Rinse the bean sprouts and drain thoroughly.

4. Heat the wok, pour in the remaining 2 tablespoons oil and heat. Stir-fry the chicken meat over a high heat, pushing it to the edge of the wok as it browns.

5. When all the meat is browned, add the curry paste, mix everything together and stir-fry for a further minute. Then add the bean sprouts and pour in the coconut milk. Cook for a further 5–6 minutes, stirring constantly.

6. Season to taste with salt and pepper and serve sprinkled with the coriander leaves.

▓ Serve with aromatic or boiled rice.

Tip
You can save time if you use a ready-made curry paste instead of making it yourself.

Lamb with red lentils

Serves 4:
500 g/1 lb boned shoulder of lamb
5 tablespoons oil
1–2 teaspoons sambal oelek
½–1 teaspoon ground cumin
½–1 teaspoon ground coriander
2 cloves garlic
1 bunch spring onions
150 g/5 oz red lentils
250 ml/8 fl oz meat stock
salt
freshly ground black pepper

Elegant

About 2100 kJ/500 kcal per portion

Preparation time: about 45 minutes
(+ 4–5 hours marinating time)

1. Wash the lamb, dry and shred or cut into cubes.

2. Mix the oil with the sambal oelek, cumin and coriander. Peel and crush the garlic. Add the meat and marinate in the refrigerator for 4–5 hours.

3. Trim and wash the spring onions and cut into thin rings. Pick over the lentils, put in a sieve and wash under the cold tap.

4. Heat the wok. Stir-fry the marinated lamb for about 3 minutes, pushing the meat to the edge of the wok as it browns.

5. Add the spring onions, lentils and stock, together with the remaining marinade. Simmer everything over a medium heat for 10 minutes, stirring frequently. Make sure that the lentils remain immersed in the stock, otherwise they will not cook. Before serving, season the lamb to taste with salt and pepper.

◼ Serve with boiled rice, and perhaps a salad or a vegetable dish.

Chicken livers with apple

Serves 4:
250 g/½ lb onions
500 g/1 lb chicken livers
3 small, sour apples
2 tablespoons lemon juice
3 tablespoons oil
200 g/7 oz cream
2 teaspoons fresh marjoram
salt
freshly ground black pepper
3–4 tablespoons dry sherry, according to taste

Economical

About 1900 kJ/450 kcal per portion

Preparation time: about 30 minutes

1. Peel the onions, halve and slice thinly.

2. Wash the chicken livers, dry and cut into bite-sized pieces, carefully removing any membrane, tubes and traces of blood.

3. Cut the apples into quarters, peel and slice. Sprinkle with the lemon juice, cover and set aside.

4. Heat the wok, pour in 2 tablespoons oil and heat. Stir-fry the onions for about 3 minutes.

5. Push the onions to the edge of the wok. Heat the last tablespoon oil in the bottom of the wok and stir-fry the chopped liver. Push the pieces to the edge when cooked.

6. Add the sliced apple and mix everything together. Pour in the cream and season with the marjoram, salt, pepper and sherry, if used. Cook everything for a further minute.

▧ Serve with mashed or boiled potatoes.

Braised chicken with water chestnuts

Serves 4:
1 large oven-ready chicken
(about ½ kg/3½ lbs)
1 bunch spring onions
50 g/2 oz fresh ginger
2 cloves garlic
4 rings fresh pineapple
200 ml/7 fl oz chicken broth
4 tablespoons rice wine
6 tablespoons soy sauce
2 teaspoons sugar
2 tablespoons oil
2 tins water chestnuts
(about 400 g/13 oz)
1–2 teaspoons cornflour

From China

About 1800 kJ/430 kcal per portion

Preparation time: about 1 hour
10 minutes

1. Skin the chicken, wash and dry. Chop into small pieces. (Or just cut into serving portions, if you are not intending to eat with chopsticks.)

2. Trim and wash the spring onions and cut into rings. Peel the ginger and garlic and chop finely.

3. Peel the pineapple rings, remove the tough centre and cut into bite-sized pieces.

4. Mix the chicken stock with the rice wine, soy sauce and sugar.

5. Heat the wok, pour in the oil and heat. Stir-fry the chicken pieces over a high heat. Briefly stir-fry the garlic, ginger and spring onions with the meat. Pour in the prepared sauce, cover and braise for about 30 minutes.

6. Drain the water chestnuts and add to the wok, together with the pineapple pieces.

7. Mix the cornflour with a little water to a smooth paste and use to thicken the sauce in the wok. Simmer everything for a further minute, then season to taste and serve.

■ Serve with rice and a hot sauce.

Chicken in basil and tomato sauce

Serves 4:
100 g/3¾ oz shallots
500 g/1 lb chicken breast fillet
750 g/1¾ lbs tomatoes
1 large bunch basil
2 tablespoons oil
200 g/7 oz crème fraîche
salt
freshly ground black pepper

Very simple

About 1600 kJ/380 kcal per portion

Preparation time: about 40 minutes

1. Peel the shallots and chop finely. Rinse the chicken breast fillets under the cold tap, dry and cut into small cubes.

2. Make incisions in the tomatoes and place briefly in boiling water. Remove and skin, then chop coarsely.

3. Wash the basil if necessary and dry thoroughly; set aside a few leaves for decoration. Cut the rest into thin strips.

4. Heat the oil, pour in the oil and heat. Stir-fry the shallots until transparent. Add the chicken meat piece by piece and stir-fry over a high heat for 1 minute. Push the meat to the edge of the wok as it browns.

5. When all the meat is browned, add the chopped tomatoes to the wok and pour in the crème fraîche Mix all the ingredients together and season with the finely chopped basil, salt and pepper. Simmer for a further 4 minutes over a high heat, stirring constantly.

6. Season the sauce to taste with salt and pepper, and serve garnished with whole basil leaves.

■ Serve with green ribbon noodles cooked al dente in plenty of salted water.

Tip
Flavour the sauce with a little wine.

Rice and noodles

Rice and Asia – in most people's minds, the two words are inextricably linked. And quite rightly so, since the white grains are eaten every day by most people in many Asian countries. But how wonderfully aromatic they are – try Thai perfumed rice – and in what sophisticated combinations they are served, not just as a side-dish! Noodles are just as versatile. All pasta fans have cause to rejoice: people in Asian countries eat noodles made not only from wheat flour but also from rice or soya bean flour. They lend themselves readily to the creation of new dishes that will make a welcome change from spaghetti with tomato sauce.

Rice should be sticky

Rice is one of the basic foodstuffs in Asia. However, it is not cooked the same way in all countries. In China, rice should be sticky and is often mixed with other ingredients. In Indonesia it is boiled first before being steamed in the rice steamer. It turns out less grainy than we are perhaps used to, and less sticky than in China. In Thailand, rice of a sticky consistency is especially popular, particularly the famous aromatic rice. And in Japan and Korea the rice is a fat short-grain variety which becomes sticky when cooked.

In foreground: Rice with eggs
In background: Rice with beans

Rice is cooked almost everywhere in Asia without salt – try it and see if you like it. You can of course add a little salt to the rice, but be careful: a lot of Asian dishes are very spicy. This section gives details of various basic cooking methods. During a lengthy meal, all types of rice can be kept warm over a pan of boiling water. To serve 4 people you will need about 250 g/8 oz rice.

Sticky rice

Put the aromatic rice in a sieve and rinse under the cold tap. Boil three times the volume of water, add the rice and stir until the water boils again. Cover and cook over a low heat for about 15 minutes until all the water is absorbed and the rice has swelled up. Salt lightly if required.

Aromatic or basmati rice

Wash 2 cups aromatic rice, changing the water until it remains clear. Bring to the boil in 3 cups water, boil for about 2 minutes then turn the heat down low. Cover and simmer for 7–8 minutes. The water should now be all absorbed and the surface of the rice should be dry. Pour boiling water over it, until the rice is covered to a depth of about ½ cm/¼ in. Cover and cook over a low heat for a further 5 minutes, then turn off the heat and leave the pan on the hob for another 7–8 minutes while the rice puffs up. Salt lightly if required.

Red beans and rice

Serves 4:
50 g/2 oz small dried red beans
250 ml/8 fl oz water
125 g/4 oz short-grain rice
salt

From Korea

About 710 kJ/170 kcal per portion

Preparation time: about 1 hour

1. Put the beans in the water, cover and cook over a low heat for about 30 minutes.

2. Add the rice and salt, cover and cook for a further 25 minutes.

Rice with eggs

Serves 4:
250 g/8 oz rice
salt
2 chicken breast fillets
(about 150 g/5 oz)
150 g/5 oz shiitake mushrooms
4 spring onions
250 ml/8 fl oz rich chicken stock
4 tablespoons light soy sauce
2 tablespoons rice wine
6 eggs

From Japan

About 1700 kJ/400 kcal per portion

Preparation time: about 45 minutes

1. Cook the rice in lightly salted water and keep warm in a covered pan.

2. Wash and dry the chicken breast fillets and cut into thin slices.

3. Trim the shiitake mushrooms, clean with a damp cloth and slice.

4. Trim and wash the spring onions and cut diagonally into rings or pieces.

5. Bring the stock to the boil in the wok and add the soy sauce and rice wine. Add the chicken meat, mushrooms and spring onion rings and cook everything for about 3 minutes.

6. Whisk the eggs lightly. Pour into the boiling stock and allow to thicken over a low heat for about 2 minutes, stirring continuously.

7. Put the rice into individual bowls and pour the stock with the meat, mushrooms, onions and eggs over it.

Fried noodles with chicken

Serves 4:
200 g/7 oz flat rice noodles
500 g/1 lb chicken breast fillets
4 tablespoons fish sauce
2 teaspoons clear honey
4 teaspoons vinegar
2 teaspoons shrimp paste
a little chilli paste or Tabasco
65 g/2½ oz unsalted peanuts
2 eggs
1 bunch spring onions
3 tablespoons oil

From Thailand

About 2100 kJ/500 kcal per portion

Preparation time: about 45 minutes

1. Place the rice noodles in a bowl, cover with hot water and leave to soak for about 30 minutes.

2. In the meantime, rinse the chicken breast fillets under the cold tap, dry and cut into thin slices.

3. Mix the fish sauce to a smooth paste with the honey, vinegar, shrimp paste and chilli paste or Tabasco.

4. Grind the peanuts finely. Whisk the eggs in a cup. Trim and wash the spring onions and cut diagonally into thin rings.

5. Heat the wok, pour in the oil and heat. Stir-fry the meat over a high heat, pushing the meat to the edge as it browns. When all the meat is browned, add the sauce.

6. Drain the noodles. Put in the wok with the spring onions and mix thoroughly for about 2 minutes.

7. Add the ground peanuts, fold in the whisked eggs and mix everything together for a further 1–2 minutes. Sprinkle with coriander leaves or parsley.

■ Serve with a spicy sauce.

Bami goreng

Serves 4:
200 g/7 oz flat rice noodles
400 g/13 oz beef fillet
2 medium-sized onions
2 cloves garlic
400 g/13 oz vegetables
(eg shiitake mushrooms, celery,
carrots, mangetout)
3 tablespoons oil
5–6 teaspoons soy sauce, depending
on taste
1 teaspoon sambal oelek

From Indonesia

About 1700 kJ/400 kcal per portion

Preparation time: about 45 minutes

1. Soak the rice noodles for about
30 minutes in plenty of warm water.

2. Rinse the beef fillet under the cold
tap, dry and shred. Peel the onions
and garlic and chop finely. Trim and
wash the vegetables and cut into thin
strips.

3. Heat the wok, pour in the oil and
heat. Stir-fry the onions and garlic
until transparent. Add the rest of the
vegetables and stir-fry everything for
about 4 minutes.

4. Push the vegetables to the edge of
the wok. Stir-fry the meat over a high
heat.

5. Mix the soy sauce with the sambal
oelek and pour into the wok. Drain the
noodles and add them to the wok. Mix
all the ingredients and stir-fry for a
further 4 minutes until the noodles are
heated through.

▨ Serve with soy sauce.

Tip
Vegetables can be chosen according to
taste and availability, and can be
varied each time you cook the dish.

Sweet and sour curried rice

Serves 4:
1 bunch spring onions
500 g/1 lb chicory
3–4 rings pineapple (about 500 g/1 lb)
4 tablespoons oil
1–1½ tablespoons curry powder
250 ml/8 fl oz stock
625 g/1½ lb boiled rice
(about 200 g/7 oz dry weight)
5 tablespoons vinegar
4–5 tablespoons soy sauce

Elegant

About 1400 kJ/330 kcal per portion

Preparation time: about 30 minutes

1. Trim and wash the spring onions and cut diagonally into thin rings. Trim and wash the chicory and slice thinly.

2. Peel the pineapple and remove the hard centre. Cut into bite-sized chunks.

3. Heat the wok, pour in the oil and heat. Stir-fry the spring onions for about 3 minutes (putting a few green rings to one side for garnishing).

4. Sprinkle the spring onions with the curry powder, fry briefly and then pour on the stock. Add the chicory and cook everything over a high heat for about 2 minutes.

5. Add the rice and pineapple, season with the vinegar and soy sauce and stir-fry for a further 4–5 minutes. Serve garnished with the green spring onion rings.

Serving tip
You could mix fried chicken or pork fillet with the rice. The curried rice could also be served as an accompaniment to meat dishes.

Rice with onions and mushrooms

Serves 4:
250 g/8 oz aromatic rice
2 bunches spring onions
400 g/13 oz small mushrooms
3 tablespoons oil
6 eggs
salt or 3 tablespoons light soy sauce
freshly ground black pepper

Economical

About 1800 kJ/430 kcal per portion

Preparation time: about 40 minutes

1. Cook the aromatic rice (see page 69), and drain if necessary.

2. Trim and wash the spring onions and cut diagonally into thin rings.

3. Trim and wash the mushrooms, then cut in half.

4. Heat the wok, pour in the oil and heat. Put aside a few green spring onion rings for use as a garnish, then brown the remaining onions in the wok. Add the mushrooms and stir-fry with the onions.

5. Add the cooked rice, mix everything thoroughly and stir-fry for a further 3 minutes.

6. Push the rice mixture to the edge of the wok. Whisk the eggs in a bowl and season with the salt or soy sauce and pepper. Pour into the middle of the wok and scramble.

7. Mix the scrambled eggs with the rice. Season to taste with salt and pepper and serve garnished with the green spring onion rings.

■ Serve with a spicy sauce.
The rice could also be served as an accompaniment to a meat or fish dish.

Steamed rice with vegetables

Serves 2:
150 g/5 oz Chinese cabbage
300 g/10 oz boiled rice
(about 100 g/3½ oz dry weight)
1 small red pepper
1 small yellow pepper
200 g/7 oz leeks
salt
freshly ground black pepper
about 750 ml/1¾ pints chicken stock
½ bunch parsley, or to taste
soy sauce or a spicy sauce, to taste

Very simple

About 540 kJ/130 kcal per portion

Preparation time: about 40 minutes

1. Trim and wash the Chinese cabbage. If you are going to use a bamboo steamer, cover the bottom with a few Chinese cabbage leaves so that the rice does not fall through the bamboo mesh.

2. Cut the rest of the cabbage into strips 1–2 cm/½–1 in across and mix with the rice.

3. Trim and wash the pepper, then cut into thin strips and mix with the rice. Trim the leeks, slit lengthways and wash thoroughly. Cut into pieces about 5 cm/2 in in length, then cut these into narrow strips and mix with the rice.

4. Season the rice with salt and pepper and place on the bed of cabbage leaves or on a shallow, heat-resistant plate.

5. Bring the stock to the boil in the wok. Put the steamer in the wok and cover with the lid. Steam the rice for about 15 minutes.

6. Wash and dry the parsley. Chop coarsely and scatter over the cooked rice. Sprinkle soy sauce over the rice at the table.

Variations
Mix 150 g/5 oz peeled, cooked shrimps or 200 g/7 oz shredded chicken meat with the rice before steaming. You can also vary the vegetables according to taste.

Tip
It is very difficult to steam larger quantities of rice evenly, because the rice and vegetables swell up too much. If you are cooking this dish for 4 people, steam the rice in 2 batches.

Nasi goreng

Serves 4:
2 large onions
2 cloves garlic
2 large red chillies
250 g/8 oz chicken breast, pork or beef fillet
100 g/3½ oz peeled, cooked shrimps
3 eggs
5–6 tablespoons soy sauce
freshly ground white pepper
4–5 tablespoons oil
400–500 g/13–16 oz boiled rice (about 150 g/5 oz uncooked)

From Java

About 1600 kJ/380 kcal per portion

Preparation time: about 1 hour

1. Peel the onions and garlic and chop finely. Trim the chillies, slit open and wash out the seeds. Cut into thin rings.

2. Rinse the meat under the cold tap, dry and shred very finely. Put the shrimps in a sieve, rinse under the cold tap and then drain thoroughly.

3. Whisk the eggs in a bowl with 3 tablespoons soy sauce and pepper.

4. Heat the wok, pour in a little oil and heat, distributing the oil evenly around the lower part of the wok. One by one, make three or four thin omelettes with the eggs, remove from the wok and cut into thin strips.

5. Heat the rest of the oil in the wok. Add the onions, garlic and chillies and stir-fry for about 1 minute.

6. Add the meat and stir-fry until browned, then add the shrimps and brown.

7. Add the rice and stir-fry for 5–7 minutes, until golden brown. Season to taste with soy sauce and pepper and mix with the strips of omelette.

The original
There are many variations of this popular Javanese dish, although rice always forms the basis.

Rice with mushrooms and tofu

Serves 4:
750 ml/1¼ pints vegetable stock
250 g/8 oz long-grain rice
1 walnut-sized piece ginger
6 tablespoons light soy sauce
¼ teaspoon sambal oelek
freshly ground black pepper
500 g/1 lb tofu
300 g/10 oz cultivated mushrooms
300 g/10 oz oyster mushrooms
4 salad onions
5 tablespoons oil
4 tablespoons freshly chopped parsley

Economical

About 2000 kJ/480 kcal per portion

Preparation time: about 1 hour

1. Bring the stock to the boil, add the rice and boil for 20 minutes until just cooked.

2. In the meantime, peel the ginger and chop finely. Mix with the soy sauce, sambal oelek and pepper. Cut the tofu into slices and then into strips. Add to the marinade, cover and put aside.

3. Trim and wash all the mushrooms and chop coarsely, leaving small ones whole. Peel and chop the onions.

4. Strain the cooked rice in a sieve, rinse with cold water and drain.

5. Heat the wok, pour in the oil and heat. Add the onions and stir-fry over a moderate heat until transparent. Add the mushrooms and stir-fry briefly with the onions.

6. Add the rice and stir-fry for a few minutes. Finally, mix in the tofu and the marinade and cook briefly. Season the mixture generously and sprinkle with parsley.

■ Goes well with a sweet and sour sauce.

Rice with leeks and smoked sausage

Serves 4:
400 g/13 oz smoked sausage (pork or beef)
625 g/1½ lb leeks
150 g/5 oz small, firm tomatoes
1 bunch parsley
4 tablespoons oil
50 g/2 oz flaked almonds
500–625 g/1–1½ lbs boiled rice
(175–200 g/6–7 oz uncooked)
salt
freshly ground black pepper

Economical

About 3400 kJ/810 kcal per portion

Preparation time: about 40 minutes

1. Cover the sausage in boiling water and leave for a few minutes. Remove from the water, dry and slice, cutting the slices in half if necessary.

2. In the meantime, trim the leeks, slit open and wash thoroughly. Cut into thin rings.

3. Wash the tomatoes and slice thinly, removing the hard end of the stalks. Wash and dry the parsley and chop finely.

4. Heat the wok, pour in the oil and heat. Add the flaked almonds, leeks and sliced sausage and stir-fry for 4 minutes.

5. Stir in the rice and stir-fry everything for a further 4–5 minutes. Finally, add the tomatoes and parsley and mix in. Season to taste with salt and pepper.

◼ You could try combining the familiar with the exotic and serve this dish with a sweet and sour sauce.

Fried noodles with prawns and mushrooms

Serves 4:
20 g/¾ oz dried shiitake mushrooms (tong koo mushrooms)
100 g/3½ oz thin rice noodles
400 g/13 oz peeled, cooked prawns
1 bunch spring onions
2 red peppers
300 g/10 oz bamboo shoots
4 tablespoons oil
4 cloves garlic
2 tablespoons white wine vinegar
4 tablespoons oyster sauce
2 teaspoons sweet soy sauce
salt
freshly ground black pepper
fresh chopped coriander leaves or parsley

Easy to cook

About 1300 kJ/310 kcal per portion

Preparation time: about 1 hour

1. Rinse the mushrooms and soak for about 10 minutes in warm water. Soak the rice noodles in hot water according to the instructions on the packet.

2. Rinse the prawns under the cold tap and drain well. Trim and wash the spring onions and cut diagonally into thin rings. Trim and wash the peppers and cut into thin strips. If necessary, cut the bamboo shoots into small pieces.

3. Drain the mushrooms, remove the stalks and cut the caps into strips.

4. Heat the wok, pour in the oil and heat. Peel and crush the garlic and stir-fry briefly in the wok. Stir in the chopped pepper and spring onions, then add the chopped mushrooms, bamboo shoots and prawns. Stir-fry for about 5 minutes.

5. Mix the vinegar with the oyster sauce, soy sauce, salt and pepper and pour into the wok.

6. Drain the noodles well, mix thoroughly with the other ingredients and stir-fry briefly. Season to taste and serve sprinkled with coriander leaves or parsley.

■ Serve with a piquant sauce.

Spicy cellophane noodles with tuna

Serves 4:
150 g/5 oz cellophane noodles
6–7 small red chillies
4 leeks
2 tablespoons oil
75 g/3 oz cashew nuts
8 tablespoons fish sauce
3 tablespoons sweet soy sauce
2 200 g/7 oz tins tuna (without oil)

Economical

About 2640 kJ/630 kcal per portion

Preparation time: about 40 minutes

1. Put the cellophane noodles in a bowl, cover with hot water and leave for about 10 minutes.

2. Trim and wash the chillies, then core and cut into very thin rings. Trim the leeks, slit open, wash and dry thoroughly, then cut into thin rings.

3. Heat the wok, pour in the oil and heat. Stir-fry the cashew nuts until golden brown, then add the chillies and leeks and stir-fry everything for a further 3 minutes.

4. Drain the cellophane noodles thoroughly, then if necessary cut with scissors into small pieces and put into the wok. Season with the fish sauce and soy sauce.

5. Drain the tuna fish, break into pieces and add to the wok. Stir-fry everything for a further 2 minutes. Season the noodles to taste and serve immediately.

Variations with meat or fresh fish
The spicy noodles can also be combined with other dishes. For example, you could stir-fry 400 g/ 13 oz chopped chicken or beef, marinated beforehand if desired, with the cashew nuts. Fresh squid or fish fillets (whiting, haddock, cod, etc) also go well with the noodles.

Fish and seafood

Fish is becoming more and more popular, for many good reasons. It is a lighter alternative to heavy meat dishes. It is healthy, easily digested and low in calories. But the chief reason, quite simply, is that fish is just delicious, although its succulent delicacy will be preserved only if it is handled carefully and not overcooked. The wok is ideal for the task. You can use it to fry fillets of fish to a turn or to steam fish so that it retains all its natural goodness. Let yourself be tempted!

Steamed red mullet with rice noodles

Serves 2:
75 g/3 oz broad rice noodles
1 bunch spring onions
2 red mullets, cleaned and scaled
(150–175 g/5–6 oz each)
salt
1 clove garlic
1 hazelnut-sized piece fresh ginger
2 tablespoons oil
125 ml/4 fl oz fish or chicken stock
2 tablespoons soy sauce
1 teaspoon sambal trassie
2–3 sprigs fresh coriander

Elegant

About 1500 kJ/360 kcal per portion

Preparation time: about 40 minutes

1. Place the rice noodles in a large bowl, cover with hot water and leave to soak for about 20 minutes. Drain.

2. In the meantime, trim and wash the spring onions and cut lengthwise into strips of about the same width as the noodles.

3. Wash and dry the red mullet. Make two or three incisions on each side of the fish. Lightly sprinkle the inside with salt.

4. Peel the garlic and ginger, chop very finely and press into the incisions and stomach cavity of the fish.

5. Heat the wok, then pour in the oil and heat over a moderate flame. Add the spring onions and stir-fry for about a minute. Then add the drained noodles and stir-fry briefly. Pour in the stock and season with the soy sauce and sambal trassie. Place the fish side by side on top, cover with the wok lid and steam for about 5 minutes.

6. Lift out the fish, mix the noodle-onion mixture thoroughly and season to taste. Spread it out on a serving dish and lay the fish on top. Chop the coriander leaves and sprinkle over the fish.

■ Serve with soy sauce or another highly seasoned sauce.

Steamed fish with ginger

Serves 2:
1 sea bass, cleaned and scaled
(about 500 g/1 lb)
40 g/1½ oz fresh ginger
salt
½ l/18 fl oz water
1 spring onion
5–6 sprigs fresh coriander
2 tablespoons light soy sauce
2 teaspoons sesame oil

Simple to prepare

About 1400 kJ/330 kcal per portion

Preparation time: about 45 minutes

1. Wash and dry the bass. Using a sharp knife, make 3 or 4 diagonal incisions on each side, cutting down to the bone.

2. Peel the ginger and chop very finely. Lightly salt the bass, then press the ginger into the incisions and stomach cavity. Lay the fish on the steaming rack.

3. Boil the water in the wok. Place the steaming rack in the wok and put the lid on tightly. Steam the bass for 8–10 minutes.

4. In the meantime, trim and wash the spring onions and cut into 5 cm/2 in pieces, then cut the pieces into thin strips. Chop the coriander leaves.

5. Lay the cooked bass on a serving dish. Sprinkle with soy sauce and sesame oil and garnish with the chopped coriander leaves and spring onion.

6. Serve with rice or noodles, a sweet and sour sauce and salad or a vegetable dish.

Steaming fish in the wok
You can also steam 2–3 smaller portions of fish. However, it is difficult to fit several whole fish into a wok at the same time, so it is better to cook an additional dish separately, or to steam several fish in succession.

Deep-fried king prawns

Serves 4:
18–20 cooked, peeled king prawns
(about 250 g/½ lb)
salt
freshly ground white pepper
2 egg whites
75 g/3 oz thin rice noodles
oil for deep-frying

From Thailand

About 710 kJ/170 kcal per portion

Preparation time: about 30 minutes

1. Slit the prawns along the back and remove the vein with a sharp, pointed knife. Then wash the prawns, dry, and season lightly with salt and pepper.

2. Whisk the egg whites and pour on to a plate. Crush the rice noodles into small pieces by hand and put on another plate. Coat the prawns first with the egg white and then with the noodles.

4. Heat the oil in the wok. Fry the prawns for 2 minutes, turning several times. Lift out and drain on kitchen paper.

■ Serve with sweet and sour or hot sauce.

Serving tip
Serve the prawns alone as a sumptuous starter or with a vegetable, rice or noodle dish as a main course.

Prawns in rice paper

Serves 4:
300 g/10 oz peeled, cooked king
prawns
3 cloves garlic
½ teaspoon ground coriander
3 tablespoons oyster sauce
freshly ground white pepper
small, round sheets of dried rice paper
(1 sheet per prawn)
yolk of 1 small egg
fat for deep-frying

Serve as a starter

About 450 kJ/110 kcal per portion

Preparation time: about 1 hour

1. Wash the prawns briefly under the
cold tap and dry thoroughly. Slit up
the back and carefully remove the
dark vein. Then make an incision on
the stomach side as well.

2. Peel and crush the garlic and mix
with the coriander, oyster sauce and
pepper. Add the prawns, cover and
leave in the refrigerator for about
½ hour.

3. Soak the sheets of rice paper
separately in a large bowl filled with
cold water for about 1 minute each.
Spread out on a kitchen towel and
wrap a prawn in each one. Brush the
edges with the whisked egg yolk and
press together firmly.

4. Heat plenty of fat for deep-frying.
Deep-fry the prawns in batches for
about 3 minutes. Lift out with tongs,
shake off the fat and drain thoroughly
on kitchen paper.

■ Serve with a sweetish piquant sauce,
rice and a salad.

Squid with shiitake mushrooms

Serves 4:
500 g/1 lb squid (fresh or deep-frozen), cleaned and ready for cooking
5 tablespoons oil
freshly ground black pepper
2 cloves garlic
250 g/8 oz fresh shiitake mushrooms
250 g/8 oz mangetout
150 ml/¼ pint strong chicken stock
1 teaspoon sambal manis
1 teaspoon cornflour
salt

Elegant

About 930 kJ/220 kcal per portion

Preparation time: about 40 minutes

1. Defrost the squid if deep-frozen. Wash thoroughly, then cut into thin rings. Chop the tentacles. Season 2 tablespoons oil with pepper. Peel and crush the garlic and marinate the squid in the oil.

2. Trim but do not wash the mushrooms if at all possible. Cut into thin strips. Wash the mangetout, trim the ends and string if necessary. Cut into 2 or 3 pieces, depending on size.

3. Mix the chicken stock with the sambal manis and cornflour.

4. Heat the wok, pour in the remaining 3 tablespoons oil and heat. Stir-fry the mangetout for about 2 minutes. Add the shiitake mushrooms, and stir-fry for about 3 minutes.

5. Push the vegetables to the edge of the wok. Put the squid in the middle of the wok and stir-fry for about 3 minutes. Pour on the stock, mix everything together, bring to the boil and cook for a further 1–2 minutes, stirring constantly. Season to taste with salt and pepper.

■ Serve with French bread or rice.

Steamed fish with vegetables

Serves 4:
500 g/1 lb fish fillets
(any firm white fish)
juice of 1 lemon
½ bunch spring onions
1 red pepper
1 clove garlic
500 g/1 lb Chinese cabbage
2 tablespoons oil
3 tablespoons soy sauce
freshly ground black pepper
125 ml/4 fl oz vegetable stock
1 teaspoon cornflour

Economical

About 840 kJ/200 kcal per portion

Preparation time: about 45 minutes

1. Rinse the fish fillets under the cold tap, dry and cut into 4 or 8 evenly sized pieces. Sprinkle with the lemon juice and place in the refrigerator.

2. Trim and wash the spring onions. Cut into pieces approximately 6 cm/2½ in long, then cut these into thin strips. Trim and wash the pepper and cut into thin strips as well. Peel and crush the garlic.

3. Trim, wash and drain the Chinese cabbage. Quarter, and then cut into strips 1–2 cm/½–1 in across.

4. Heat the wok, pour in the oil and heat. Stir-fry the onion, pepper and garlic for about 3 minutes.

5. Add the Chinese cabbage and stir-fry the vegetables for a further 2–3 minutes.

6. Season the vegetables with the soy sauce and pepper. Mix the stock with the cornflour and pour into the wok. Place the pieces of fish side by side as far as possible on top of the vegetables and season with pepper. Put the lid on the wok and steam the fish over a low heat for about 6 minutes. Serve the fish with the vegetables.

■ Serve with rice or Chinese noodles.

Do not cut the fish too deeply.

Serves 2:
1 bream (about 500 g/1 lb),
cleaned and scaled
1–2 tablespoons flour
20 g/¾ oz fresh galingale or ginger
2 cloves garlic
2 small red chillies
1 bunch spring onions
2 teaspoons palm or brown sugar
2 tablespoons soy sauce
1 tablespoon rice vinegar
1 tablespoon fish sauce
100 ml/3½ fl oz water
1 teaspoon cornflour
oil for deep-frying

For special occasions

About 1600 kJ/380 kcal per portion

Preparation time: about 50 minutes

1. Wash and dry the bream, then with a sharp knife make 2 or 3 diagonal incisions on each side. Coat with flour, then shake to dispose of any excess.

2. Peel the galingale or ginger for the sauce and cut into very thin strips. Peel the garlic and chop finely. Slit open the chillies, trim, wash and seed, then cut into very thin rings.

3. Trim and wash the spring onions and cut diagonally into very thin rings.

4. Rub the palm sugar between your fingers, then mix to a smooth paste with the soy sauce, vinegar, fish sauce, water and cornflour.

5. Heat plenty of oil in the wok over a moderate flame. Fry the bream for about 10 minutes until golden brown, turning carefully several times and covering with oil on each occasion. Lift out when cooked and keep warm on a serving dish.

6. Pour most of the oil out of the wok, leaving just 1 tablespoon behind. Stir-fry the ginger, garlic and chilli for about ½ minute.

7. Set aside a few green onion rings; stir-fry the rest in the wok for 1–2 minutes.

8. Stir the prepared sauce, pour into the wok and bring everything to the boil.

9. Pour the sauce over and around the fish. Garnish with the uncooked spring onion rings.

■ Serve with rice or Chinese noodles.

Tip
Larger fish are difficult to cook in a wok. If you want to make this dish for 4 people, prepare an additional vegetable, rice or noodle dish.

Halibut with rhubarb

Serves 4:
625 g/1½ lb halibut fillets
4 tablespoons lemon juice
freshly ground white pepper
2 bunches spring onions
300 g/10 oz rhubarb
2 red chillies
8 tablespoons light soy sauce
1 teaspoon ground ginger
3 teaspoons sugar
2 cloves garlic
4 tablespoons oil

Economical

About 1100 kJ/260 kcal per portion

Preparation time: about 40 minutes

1. Wash the halibut under the cold tap, dry thoroughly and cut into bite-sized pieces. Sprinkle with the lemon juice, season with pepper, cover and place in the refrigerator.

2. Trim and wash the spring onions. Dice the white parts finely and cut the green parts diagonally into 1 cm/½ in rings. Trim the rhubarb, peel and cut into 1 cm/½ in pieces.

3. Trim and wash the chillies, deseed and cut into very thin rings. Mix with the soy sauce, ginger, sugar and pepper. Peel and crush the garlic and add to the sauce.

4. Heat the wok, pour in the oil and heat. Briefly fry the white parts of the onions, then add the rhubarb and stir-fry for 4–5 minutes.

5. Mix in the green parts of the onions, then pour in the sauce. Carefully mix in the fish, cover the wok with the lid and braise everything for a further 5 minutes.

▊ Serve with rice or French bread.

Steamed salmon

Serves 2:
2 salmon steaks
(each about 200 g/7 oz)
2 tablespoons lime or lemon juice
salt
freshly ground white pepper
a few Chinese cabbage leaves
125 g/4 fl oz fish stock
25 g/1 oz butter straight from
the refrigerator
fresh dill

For special occasions

About 2200 kJ/520 kcal per portion

Preparation time: about 30 minutes

1. Carefully wash and dry the salmon steaks. Sprinkle with the lime or lemon juice and season with salt and pepper.

2. Wash and trim the Chinese cabbage leaves and use to line a bamboo steamer. Place the salmon steaks side by side on top.

3. Bring the fish stock to the boil, put the steamer in the wok and cover with the lid. Steam the salmon steak over a moderate heat for about 3 minutes, then turn and steam for a further 3 minutes.

4. Lift the bamboo steamer out of the wok and put to one side. Pour the stock into the wok and reduce over a high flame to half its volume. Take the wok off the stove.

5. Cut the butter into small pieces and whisk into the fish stock until the sauce thickens. Stir in a few sprigs of dill, season to taste and serve with the salmon steaks.

▨ Serve with boiled potatoes and salad or steamed vegetables.

Sweet and sour haddock

Serves 4:
500 g/1 lb haddock fillets
1–2 cloves garlic
1 hazelnut-sized piece ginger
4 tablespoons sweet soy sauce
4 tablespoons light, salty soy sauce
5 tablespoons rice or white wine vinegar
¼–½ teaspoon sambal oelek
freshly ground black pepper
1 bunch spring onions
1 small fresh pineapple
(about 500 g/1 lb)
3 tablespoons oil
50 g/2 oz cashew nuts

Very simple

About 1200 kJ/290 kcal per portion

Preparation time: about 45 minutes

1. Wash the haddock fillets briefly under the cold tap, dry and cut into bite-sized pieces.

2. Peel the garlic and ginger and chop finely.

3. Mix both sorts of soy sauce with the vinegar, sambal oelek, pepper, garlic and ginger, pour over the fish, cover and place in the refrigerator.

4. Trim and wash the spring onions and cut into very thin rings. Peel and dice the pineapple (reserving any juice) and remove the hard centre.

5. Heat the wok, pour in the oil and heat. Stir-fry the cashew nuts until golden brown, then remove from the wok.

6. Put the spring onions into the wok (setting aside a few green rings for garnishing) and stir-fry for about 2 minutes.

7. Add the chopped pineapple, together with the juice, and stir briefly. Then add the marinaded fish and the marinade. Stir, cover and cook for about 4 minutes, stirring carefully once more.

8. Sprinkle with the cashew nuts and spring onion rings and serve.

■ Serve with rice.

Fried fish in sweet and sour sauce

Serves 4:
500 g/1 lb fish fillets
(cod, haddock or coley)
1 teaspoon ground ginger
1 teaspoon salt
2 egg whites
4–5 fresh red chillies
1 small tin pickled Chinese vegetables
(200 g/7 oz; gherkins,
ginger, carrots, lettuce)
250 ml/8 fl oz water
2 tablespoons sugar
4 tablespoons light soy sauce
5–6 tablespoons cornflour
oil for deep-frying

Elegant

About 740 kJ/180 kcal per portion

Preparation time: about 45 minutes

1. Rinse the fish fillets under the cold tap, dry and cut into 5 cm/2 in pieces.

2. Sprinkle the fish pieces with the ginger and salt. Lightly whip the egg whites and pour over the fish. Cover and put in the refrigerator.

3. Trim, deseed and wash the chillies and cut into very thin rings.

4. Drain the tinned vegetables, reserving the liquid. Chop the vegetables into thin strips. Mix the liquid with the water, sugar and soy sauce and stir in 2 teaspoons cornflour.

5. Heat plenty of oil in the wok. Coat the fish pieces in the remaining cornflour, then deep-fry in batches for about 2 minutes, turning occasionally, until golden brown. Remove from the fat with a skimmer and drain on kitchen paper.

6. When all the fish is cooked, pour the oil out of the wok. Stir the prepared sauce once more, then pour into the wok. Add the chilli rings and chopped vegetables, bring everything to the boil, season to taste and serve with the fish.

■ Serve with Chinese noodles or rice.

Variation
Instead of the pickled vegetables, cook a small carrot, a piece of cucumber and a little fresh ginger in salted water until soft and season with vinegar.

Steamed plaice rolls

Serves 4:
4 plaice fillets (about 500 g/1 lb)
2 tablespoons lemon juice
3 spring onions
1 clove garlic
1 hazelnut-sized piece fresh ginger
2 tablespoons black bean sauce
¾ teaspoon sambal oelek
1 tablespoon soy sauce
1 egg white
4 sticks crab meat
(or 4 peeled, cooked king prawns)
½ l/18 fl oz water

Low in calories

About 480 kJ/110 kcal per portion

Preparation time: about 40 minutes

1. Wash the plaice fillets under the cold tap, dry and sprinkle with the lemon juice. Cover and place in the refrigerator.

2. Trim and wash the spring onions. Cut 2 spring onions diagonally into thin rings and put aside.

3. Peel the garlic and ginger and chop very finely with the third spring onion. Mix with the black bean sauce, the sambal oelek and soy sauce.

4. Lightly whisk the egg white. Spread out the fish fillets and coat with the egg white. Place some of the bean sauce on each fillet, together with 1 stick crab meat or 1 king prawn. Roll up the fillets, secure with cocktail sticks and place side by side on a steaming rack.

5. Bring the water to the boil in the wok. Put the steaming rack in, cover the wok and steam the plaice fillets for 5–6 minutes.

6. Scatter the spring onion rings on a serving dish. Lift the cooked plaice fillets out of the wok, cut into slices and serve on the bed of spring onions.

▇ Serve with a sour, spicy sauce, rice or noodles and vegetables.

Steamed fish in spinach

Serves 4:
400–500 g/13 oz–1 lb coley fillets
4–5 cloves garlic
6 tablespoons fish sauce
4 teaspoons five-spice powder
2 eggs
4 teaspoons sesame oil
200 g/7 oz canned bamboo shoots
40 large spinach leaves
¾ l/1¾ pints water

Low in calories

About 970 kJ/230 kcal per portion

Preparation time: about 1 hour

1. Briefly rinse the coley fillets under the cold tap, dry and shred finely.

2. Peel and finely chop the garlic and mix with the fish sauce, five-spice powder, eggs and sesame oil. Marinate the fish in this mixture.

3. Drain the bamboo shoots, cut into thin strips and mix with the fish.

4. Trim and wash the spinach leaves and blanch in boiling water. Drain thoroughly, spread out on a work surface and pat dry with kitchen paper.

5. Put a little of the filling on each of the spinach leaves and roll up the leaves, turning the sides of each leaf inwards so that the filling is enclosed.

6. Lay the rolled leaves side by side in a bamboo steamer or on a heat-resistant plate and place in the wok. Pour the water into the wok from the side, bring the water to the boil and cover the wok. Steam over a moderate heat for about 7 minutes.

■ Serve with a sweet and sour dip and rice.

Creole prawns

Serves 4:
3 onions
4 cloves garlic
3 cm/1½ in piece fresh ginger
2–3 small red chillies
750 g/1½ lbs tomatoes
3 tablespoons oil
1 small packet ground saffron
1 teaspoon grated lemon peel
1 teaspoon curry powder
1 teaspoon dried thyme
salt
freshly ground black pepper
16–20 cooked king prawns (peeled except for the tail)
1 teaspoon freshly chopped parsley

Highly seasoned

About 830 kJ/200 kcal per portion

Preparation time: about 45 minutes

1. Peel the onions and dice finely. Peel the garlic and ginger and chop finely.

2. Slit open the chillies and wash out the seeds. Cut into paper-thin rings.

3. Make incisions in the tomato skins and place briefly in boiling water. Lift out, skin and chop finely.

4. Heat the wok, pour in the oil and heat. Stir-fry the onions until transparent, the stir in the garlic, ginger and chillies and stir-fry with the onions.

5. Stir in the saffron, lemon peel, curry powder and thyme, then add the tomatoes. Season the vegetables with salt and pepper and simmer over a low heat for about 10 minutes; add a little water if necessary.

6. Rinse the prawns under the cold tap and add to the tomato mixture. Cook everything for 3–4 minutes – the prawns should just be heated through. Season the sauce to taste, sprinkle with the parsley and serve immediately.

■ Serve with rice and a hot chilli sauce.

Curried prawns

Serves 4:
200 g/7 oz fresh baby corn (or a 400 g/13 oz can)
1 bunch spring onions
2 cloves garlic
1 hazelnut-sized piece fresh ginger
300 g/10 oz cooked, peeled prawns
3–4 teaspoons curry paste
6 tablespoons fish sauce
4 tablespoons light soy sauce
200 g/7 oz coconut milk (see page 24)
2 teaspoons sugar
3 tablespoons oil
6–8 kaffir lime leaves, cut into thin strips

From Thailand • Spicy

About 840 kJ/200 kcal per portion

Preparation time: about 50 minutes

1. Wash the baby corn, then cook in a covered pan in lightly salted water for about 7 minutes. Drain thoroughly.

2. Trim and wash the spring onions and cut into 1 cm/½ in rings. Peel the garlic and ginger and chop finely.

3. Put the prawns in a sieve, rinse under the cold tap and drain thoroughly.

4. Mix the curry paste with the fish sauce, soy sauce, coconut milk and sugar.

5. Heat the wok, pour in the oil and heat. Stir-fry the garlic and ginger briefly, then add the spring onions and stir-fry for about 1 minute.

6. Add the baby corn and stir-fry for about 2 minutes. Then stir in the prawns and fry briefly. Pour in the curry sauce and cook everything for a further 3 minutes, stirring constantly.

7. Sprinkle the curry with finely chopped lime leaves and serve.

■ Serve with aromatic rice.

Vegetables and tofu

The times are long past when broccoli and cabbage were boiled to a soft pulpy mass like baby food. Beans and carrots cooked al dente so as to be firm when eaten are now the order of the day. Not only is this the best way of retaining the flavour of vegetables, but it also means that the many valuable vitamins they contain are not destroyed during cooking. With a wok, splendid vegetable dishes can be cooked in the twinkling of an eye. They can be served as elegant main courses, perhaps supplemented with tofu, or as an accompaniment to sophisticated fish or meat dishes.

Stir-fried vegetables

Serves 4:
20 g/¾ oz dried tong koo mushrooms
1 red pepper
4 small carrots (about 200 g/7 oz)
4 spring onions
200 g/7 oz Chinese cabbage
150 g/5 oz fresh bean sprouts
3 tablespoons oil
4 cloves garlic
5 tablespoons light soy sauce
sugar
ground ginger

From Thailand

About 450 kJ/110 kcal per portion

Preparation time: about 45 minutes

1. Soak the dried mushrooms in warm water for about 30 minutes.

2. In the meantime, prepare all the vegetables. Cut the pepper in half, trim, wash and cut into thin strips. Trim and wash the carrots and spring onions and cut diagonally into thin strips. Trim and wash the Chinese cabbage, dry thoroughly and cut into strips 1 cm/½ in across. Wash and drain the bean sprouts.

3. Squeeze the mushrooms dry, cut off the stems and chop into fairly small pieces.

4. Heat the wok, pour in the oil and heat. Peel and crush the garlic and stir-fry with the pepper and carrots for about 2 minutes.

5. Add the mushrooms and spring onions and stir-fry for a further 2 minutes, then stir in the Chinese cabbage and bean sprouts. Cook everything for a further 3 minutes.

6. Season the vegetables with the soy sauce, sugar and ground ginger.

Serving tip
Serve as an accompaniment to meat or fish dishes, supplemented with potatoes, noodles, rice or bread, according to taste. Or you could first stir-fry small pieces of meat, take them out of the wok and then mix them in again when the vegetables are cooked.

Vegetables in curry sauce

Serves 4:
200 g/7 oz fresh baby corn
(or 400 g/13 oz tin)
salt
250 g/8 oz carrots
1 bunch thin, tender spring onions
100 g/3½ oz fresh bean sprouts
2 cloves garlic
1 walnut-sized piece fresh ginger
3 teaspoons curry paste
5 tablespoons fish sauce
5 tablespoons soy sauce
200 ml/7 fl oz coconut milk (see page 24)
2 teaspoons sugar
3 tablespoons oil
5 kaffir lime leaves, cut into thin strips

Hot

About 670 kJ/160 kcal per portion

Preparation time: about 40 minutes

1. Wash the fresh baby corn, then cook covered in lightly salted water for about 7 minutes. Drain well.

2. Trim, wash and peel the carrots and cut into matchstick-sized strips.

3. Trim and wash the spring onions and cut into pieces the same length as the baby corn.

4. Place the bean sprouts in a sieve and rinse under the cold tap. Drain well.

5. Peel the garlic and ginger and chop finely.

6. Mix the curry paste with the fish sauce, soy sauce, coconut milk and sugar.

7. Heat the wok, pour in the oil and heat. Stir-fry the garlic and ginger briefly, then add the carrots and baby corn and stir-fry everything for about 2 minutes. Mix in the spring onions and stir-fry for a further 2 minutes.

8. Pour on the curry sauce and cook everything for a further 3 minutes, stirring constantly. Sprinkle with chopped lime leaves and serve.

▨ Serve with rice or noodles and a meat or fish dish.

Serving tip
These curried vegetable make a splendid accompaniment to many dishes, for example steamed fish. With the addition of small pieces of stir-fried meat, it could be served as a main dish.

Broccoli in oyster sauce

Serves 4:
1 kg/2 lbs broccoli
salt
6 cloves garlic
8 tablespoons oyster sauce
freshly ground black pepper
1 teaspoon cornflour
100 ml/3½ fl oz water
4 tablespoons oil

Elegant

About 670 kJ/160 kcal per portion

Preparation time: about 30 minutes

1. Trim and wash the broccoli. Cut off the stems and chop into small pieces. Divide the florets into bite-sized pieces. Blanch the broccoli in lightly salted water for about 1 minute, drain and rinse in cold water to stop it cooking any further.

2. Peel the garlic and crush or chop it. Mix the oyster sauce with pepper, cornflour and water to a smooth paste.

3. Heat the oil in the wok and stir-fry the garlic briefly. Add the broccoli and stir-fry briefly, then pour on the sauce. Stir-fry everything for 1–2 minutes and season to taste with pepper.

■ Serve with fried or steamed meat or fish. Supplement with noodles or rice.

Stir-fried celery

Serves 4:
1 large head celery
(about 750 g/1½ lbs)
2 tablespoons sweet bean sauce
4 tablespoons ketjap manis or soy
sauce
4 tablespoons rice wine
2 tablespoons oil
cayenne pepper

Quick to prepare

About 300 kJ/70 kcal per portion

Preparation time: about 20 minutes

1. Trim and wash the celery, retaining
the leaves. Cut the celery sticks into
pieces about 1 cm/½ in across; chop
the leaves.

2. Mix the bean sauce with the ketjap
manis and rice wine.

3. Heat the wok, pour in the oil and
heat. Stir-fry the celery over a
moderate heat for about 6 minutes.

4. Pour in the sauce, add the celery
leaves and mix everything thoroughly.
Season to taste with cayenne pepper.

■ Serve with spicy fish dishes, and
supplement with rice or noodles.

Stir-fried tofu with sesame seeds

Serves 4:
500 g/1 lb tofu
4 tablespoons flour
2 eggs
125 g/4 oz peeled sesame seeds
6 tablespoons oil
For the sauce:
5 tablespoons rice wine
5 tablespoons rice vinegar
100 ml/3½ fl oz soy sauce
1 teaspoon freshly ground black pepper
1 teaspoon sugar

From Japan

About 2100kJ/500 kcal per portion

Preparation time: about 30 minutes

1. Drain the tofu and cut into pieces 1 cm/½ in thick and then into strips about 2 cm/1 in across and 5 cm/2 in in length.

2. Sprinkle the flour onto a plate. Whisk the eggs in a small bowl. Place the sesame seeds on another plate. Dip the tofu first in the flour, then in the egg and finally in the sesame seeds.

3. Mix the sauce ingredients together.

4. Pour the oil into the wok and heat to a moderate temperature. Gradually add the tofu and stir-fry carefully for 3–5 minutes. Lift out the tofu pieces as they cook and keep warm.

5. Serve the fried tofu pieces with the sauce.

■ Serve with rice or noodles and vegetables.

Variation: Stir-fried tofu with sesame seeds and steamed rice with vegetables
You can also serve the tofu as a main course. Fry the tofu as decribed above and then remove from the wok. Stir-fry some chopped vegetables in a little oil, then after a little while (depending on the vegetables) add some boiled rice and stir-fry. Carefully mix in the tofu and serve.

Tofu with mushrooms

Serves 4:
500 g/1 lb tofu
125 ml/4 fl oz strong vegetable stock
grated rind from a lemon
freshly ground black pepper
1 bunch parsley
400 g/13 oz button mushrooms
2 small, firm tomatoes
1 medium-sized onion
3–4 tablespoons flour
4 tablespoons oil
salt

Low in calories

About 950 kJ/230 kcal per portion

Preparation time: about 40 minutes
(+ at least 1 hour marinating time)

1. Drain the tofu and cut first into pieces ½ cm/¼ in thick and then into strips about 2 cm/1 in across.

2. Season the stock well with lemon peel and pepper. Wash and dry the parsley, chop finely and add to the stock. Add the tofu, cover and leave to marinate for at least 1 hour.

3. Trim and wash the mushrooms, or rub with a damp cloth. Cut in half or into thickish slices. Wash the tomatoes and slice, removing the woody parts at the top.

4. Peel the onions and chop finely.

5. Drain the tofu, retaining the marinade. Sprinkle the flour onto a plate and coat the tofu in it.

6. Heat the wok, pour in 1 tablespoon oil and heat. Add the onions and stir-fry until transparent. Gradually add the strips of tofu and brown in the middle of the wok, pushing each one to the edge as soon as it browns. Keep adding a little oil to the wok as you fry the tofu.

7. When all the tofu has been browned, stir-fry the mushrooms. Pour in the marinade, add the tomatoes and carefully mix all the ingredients together. Heat through and season to taste with salt and pepper.

■ Serve with rice noodles or rice.

Stir-fried courgettes with parsley

Serves 4:
750 g/1½ lb courgettes
2 bunches parsley
3 tablespoons oil
salt
freshly ground black pepper
freshly grated nutmeg

Very simple

About 370 kJ/88 kcal per portion

Preparation time: about 25 minutes

1. Trim and wash the courgettes. Cut first into slices ½ cm/¼ in thick, then into strips about the same width.

2. Wash and dry the parsley and chop finely, removing the coarse stems.

3. Heat the wok, pour in the oil and heat. Add the chopped courgettes and stir-fry for about 4 minutes.

4. Mix in the parsley and season with salt, pepper and a little nutmeg.

Serving tip
Serve with roast meat or steamed fish. You can choose the accompanying dish according to taste and occasion; potatoes go just as well with it as rice or bread.

Variation
The addition of boiled rice or possibly a little diced cooked ham will make this a satisfying main course.

Creamy cabbage with bacon

Serves 4:
150 g/5 oz smoked streaky bacon
1 onion
750 g/1½ lb savoy (or Chinese) cabbage
2 tablespoons oil
25 g/1 oz unpeeled sesame seeds
150 ml/¼ pint chicken stock
salt
freshly ground black pepper
150 g/5 oz crème fraîche

Economical

About 2200kJ/520 kcal per portion

Preparation time: about 30 minutes

1. Cut the bacon into thin strips, discarding the rind. Peel and chop the onion.

2. Trim, wash and dry the cabbage. Divide into 8 equal parts, cut out the hard centre and chop each part into strips 1 cm/½ in across.

3. Heat the wok, pour in the oil and heat. Brown the bacon. Add the chopped onion and brown slightly.

4. Stir in the prepared cabbage and stir-fry for about 5 minutes. Finally, add the sesame seeds and stir-fry briefly with the other ingredients.

5. Pour in the stock. Season the cabbage with salt and pepper, cover and steam for about 5 minutes.

6. Stir in the crème fraîche and heat through. Season the cabbage to taste.

■ Serve as an accompaniment to flash-fried meat or grilled fish.

Variation
For a main course, add 400 g/13 oz boiled wheat grains (about 150 g/5 oz uncooked weight) and pour on a little more stock.

Bean sprouts with peppers

Serves 4:
300 g/10 oz fresh bean sprouts
1 green pepper
1 red pepper
2 tablespoons oil
2 tablespoons sweet soy sauce
freshly ground black pepper

Rich in vitamins

About 320 kJ/76 kcal per portion

Preparation time: about 30 minutes

1. Wash and pick over the bean sprouts. Leave to drain in a sieve.

2. Cut the peppers in half and core. Wash and cut into very thin strips.

3. Heat the wok, pour in the oil and heat. Stir-fry the chopped peppers.

4. Add the bean sprouts and season with the soy sauce and pepper. Stir-fry for a further 2 minutes.

Serving tip
Particularly good as an accompaniment to flash-fried meat. Serve with fried potatoes and salad or as part of a substantial meal cooked in the wok and featuring several specialities.

Braised Chinese cabbage with bean sprouts

Serves 4:
1 Chinese cabbage
(about 750 g/1½ lbs)
300 g/10 oz fresh bean sprouts
3 cm/1½ in piece fresh ginger
4 tablespoons soya oil
4 tablespoons soy sauce
100 ml/3½ fl oz vegetable stock
2 teaspoons sugar
salt
freshly ground black pepper
2 teaspoons sesame oil

Economical

About 580 kJ/140 kcal per portion

Preparation time: about 30 minutes

1. Trim the Chinese cabbage, removing the hard centre and discarding the outer leaves. Wash, shake dry, cut into four lengthwise and then cut each quarter crosswise into strips 1 cm/½ in across. Put the bean sprouts in a sieve, rinse under the cold tap, drain and pick over.

2. Peel the ginger and chop finely. Heat the wok, pour in the oil and heat to a moderate temperature. Stir-fry the ginger.

3. Add the Chinese cabbage and stir-fry for 6 minutes.

4. Mix in the bean sprouts. Add the soy sauce, stock and sugar, mix everything together and cook for a further 5 minutes. Season to taste with salt and pepper, sprinkle with the sesame oil and serve.

▦ Serve with rice and a spicy meat dish.

Variation
For a less "exotic" dish, substitute a chopped onion for the ginger. Season with salt and pepper only, leaving out the sesame oil.

Stir-fried vegetables with turmeric

Serves 4:
1 cucumber (500 g/1 lb)
400 g/13 oz carrots
2 medium-sized onions
4 cloves garlic
1 teaspoon sambal oelek
1 teaspoon turmeric
3 tablespoons oil
200 ml/7 fl oz water
3 tablespoons cashew nuts
sugar
salt
vinegar

From Indonesia

About 640 kJ/150 kcal per portion

Preparation time: about 35 minutes

1. Peel the cucumber, cut in half lengthwise and remove the seeds. Peel and wash the carrots. Cut the vegetables into thin strips.

2. Peel the onions and garlic and chop coarsely. Purée with the sambal oelek and turmeric.

3. Heat the oil in the wok to a moderate temperature and briefly stir-fry the spice mixture.

4. Add the carrots and stir-fry briefly. Then add 100 ml/3½ fl oz water and cook the carrots for about 5 minutes, stirring frequently.

5. Add the cucumber, pour in another 100 ml/3½ fl oz water and cook everything for a further 5 minutes.

6. Coarsely chop the cashew nuts and mix in with the vegetables. Season to taste with sugar, salt and vinegar.

▨ Particularly good as an accompaniment to steamed fish dishes. Serve with rice.

Spicy beans

Serves 4:
500 g/1 lb green beans
salt
250 g/½ lb tomatoes
3 cloves garlic
6 small red chillies
150 g/5 oz small onions
2 teaspoons palm or brown sugar
5 tablespoons coconut milk
(see page 24)
1 teaspoon ground galingale
2 tablespoons oil

From Java

About 480 kJ/110 kcal per portion

Preparation time: about 40 minutes

1. Trim and wash the beans and cut diagonally into 1 cm/½ in pieces. Boil for about 5 minutes in salted water, then pour into a sieve and leave to drain thoroughly.

2. Wash the tomatoes and cut each one into eight, discarding the woody parts at the top.

3. Peel the garlic. Trim the chillies, slit open lengthwise and remove the seeds. Slice the garlic and chillies as thinly as possible.

4. Peel and halve the onions, then slice thinly.

5. Rub the palm sugar between your fingers, then mix with the coconut milk and galingale.

6. Heat the wok, pour in the oil and heat. Stir-fry the garlic, chillies and onion for about 1 minute.

7. Stir in the beans and tomatoes and add the coconut sauce. Cover and steam the vegetables over a moderate heat for 5–10 minutes until the beans are cooked but are not too soft.

Serving tip
Serve with rice. Goes well with meat or fish dishes.

111

Lentil curry

Serves 4:
250 g/½ lb red lentils
salt
freshly ground black pepper
1 bunch spring onions
3 cloves garlic
4 red chillies
2 red peppers
2 tablespoons clarified butter
1–2 tablespoons curry powder

From India

About 1200 kJ/290 kcal per portion

Preparation time: about 40 minutes

1. Pick over the lentils thoroughly (there are often small stones in them) and wash. Bring to the boil in 600 ml/1 pint of cold water, add salt and pepper, cover and cook for just 10 minutes.

2. In the meantime, trim and wash the spring onions and cut into rings about ½ cm/¼ in thick. Peel the garlic and chop finely. Trim the chillies, slit open lengthwise, remove the seeds and cut into paper-thin rings.

3. Cut the peppers in half and core. Wash and cut into thin strips.

4. Heat the wok, add the clarified butter and heat. Stir-fry the spring onions, garlic, chillies and peppers for 2 minutes.

5. Sprinkle the curry powder over the vegetables and stir-fry briefly. Add the boiled lentils and the cooking liquid. Mix everything together and heat through. Season with salt and pepper and serve hot.

Variation
Stir-fry chopped lamb or pork with the vegetables before adding the lentils.

Mushrooms in rice wine

Serves 4:
100 g/3½ oz dried tong koo mushrooms (shiitake mushrooms)
400 ml/14 fl oz hot water
1 bunch spring onions
2 tablespoons oil
4 teaspoons sugar
100 ml/3½ fl oz rice wine
5 tablespoons light soy sauce
½ teaspoon cornflour

Elegant

About 470 kJ/110 kcal per portion

Preparation time: about 45 minutes

1. Soak the dried mushrooms in the water for about 30 minutes.

2. Remove the mushrooms from the water, and set the water aside. If necessary, chop the mushrooms into smaller pieces, removing and discarding the stems.

3. Trim and wash the spring onions. Cut into 5 cm/2 in pieces and cut these lengthwise into thin strips.

4. Heat the wok, pour in the oil and heat. Stir-fry the spring onions and mushrooms for about 4 minutes.

5. Mix the water used to soak the mushrooms to a smooth paste with the sugar, rice wine, soy sauce and cornflour and pour into the wok. Cook the vegetables for a further 4 minutes until the sauce thickens a little.

■ Serve as an accompaniment to steamed fish or poultry dishes.

Variation
You can of course also use fresh shiitake mushrooms for this dish. Buy about 625 g/1½ lbs. You could use ordinary cultivated mushrooms as a cheaper alternative, but they are not as aromatic.

Paksoi with sesame seeds

Serves 4:
2 heads paksoi (about 750 g/1½ lbs)
2 cloves garlic
1 walnut-sized piece fresh ginger
2 red chillies
2 tablespoons unflavoured vegetable oil
40 g/1½ oz unpeeled sesame seeds
5 tablespoons soy sauce
4–5 tablespoons water
freshly ground black pepper
2 teaspoons sesame oil

Elegant

About 660 kJ/160 kcal per portion
Preparation time: about 30 minutes

1. Trim, wash and dry the paksoi. Cut the leaves crosswise into strips 1 cm/½ in across.

2. Peel the garlic and ginger and chop very finely. Trim, core and wash the chillies and cut into paper-thin strips.

3. Heat the wok, pour in the oil and heat. Stir-fry the garlic, ginger and chillies for about 1 minute.

4. Stir in the sesame seeds, then add the paksoi and stir-fry for 3 minutes.

5. Pour in the soy sauce and water. Season the vegetables with pepper. Sprinkle with the sesame oil and serve.

▪ Particularly good as an accompaniment to steamed fish.

Stir-fried kohlrabi with basil

Serves 4:
2 small stems kohlrabi
(about 500 g/1 lb)
625 g/1¼ lbs baby carrots
250 g/½ lb mozzarella
2–3 bunches basil, depending on size
4 tablespoons oil
4 tablespoons pine kernels
salt
freshly ground black pepper
a pinch sugar

Elegant

About 1500 kJ/360 kcal per portion

Preparation time: about 45 minutes

1. Peel the kohlrabi, setting aside any tender leaves. Cut each stem first into thin slices and then into thin strips.

2. Peel the carrots and cut into thin strips. Drain the mozzarella and cut into strips.

3. Wash and dry the basil. Pick off the leaves and cut into strips. Finely chop the kohlrabi leaves and mix with the chopped basil.

4. Heat the wok, pour in the oil and heat. Add the vegetables and stir-fry for about 8 minutes. Push the vegetables to the edge and then brown the pine kernels briefly in the middle of the wok.

5. Add the chopped basil and kohlrabi leaves and the mozzarella, mix everything together and fry very briefly. Season with salt, pepper and sugar.

■ Serve with noodles. If desired, add pieces of meat or fish and stir-fry with the vegetables.

Index

Angelika Ilies

A native of Hamburg now living in Munich, she is a dedicated and successful freelance writer and food journalist. As soon as she had completed her studies in domestic economy and nutrition, she launched her career, beginning in London, where she worked for a famous publishing house, learning all about the book trade and at the same time sampling the wide range of international cuisines on offer in the city. On her return to Germany, she worked for four and a half years in the cookery section of the largest German food magazine; since 1989 she has been earning her daily bread as a freelance writer.

"Foodfotografie Eising"

was founded in 1980 by Pete A. Eising and Susanne Eising. The studio specializes exclusively in high-quality food and drink photography. Its clients include advertising agencies, food companies, magazines and publishing houses producing cookery books. The studio employs a team of professional photographers and food stylists as well as two full-time cooks. To complete the service offered by the studio, it also runs a picture agency with offices in Munich and Switzerland, which also of course specialises in food.